UNFAIR DISMISSAL

EMPLOYMENT LAW GUIDES

PRACTICAL GUIDES TO LAW AT WORK

Other titles in the series:

A Guide to the Employment Acts
Joan Henderson

Handling Redundancy
Sue Morris

Industrial Tribunals – How to Present your Case
Philip Parry

Statutory Maternity Pay and Maternity Rights
Gillian Howard (revised by Sue Morris)

Statutory Sick Pay
Gillian Howard (revised by Sue Morris)

*The Work Environment – The Law of Health,
Safety and Welfare*
Patricia Leighton

THE INDUSTRIAL SOCIETY

The Industrial Society is an independent, self-financing organisation with charitable status.

The Society works to develop the full talents and potential of people at work, and those seeking work, and to increase employee involvement and personal fulfilment through work.

The Industrial Society meets these objectives by identifying good practice at work and successful new approaches. These are promoted through courses and conferences, advice, training, information and publications. The Society works in all sectors to guide people towards finding practical solutions which will achieve results in their organisation.

UNFAIR DISMISSAL
YOUR LEGAL RIGHTS

RICHARD W PAINTER

First published 1991 by
The Industrial Society Press
Robert Hyde House
48 Bryanston Square
London W1H 7LN
Telephone: 071 262 2401

British Library cataloguing-in-publication data
Painter, Richard W.
  Unfair dismissal – your legal rights.
  (Employment law guides)
  I. Title   II. Series
  344.42

ISBN 0 85290 915 2

Cover design by Oliver Relfe

Typeset by Acūté, Stroud, Glos.
Printed by The Lavenham Press Limited

CONTENTS

TABLE OF STATUTES AND REGULATIONS

Access to Medical Reports Act 1988

Employment Acts 1980, 1982, 1988, 1989, 1990

Employment Protection Act 1975

Employment Protection (Consolidation) Act 1978

Employment Protection (Recoupment of Unemployment Benefit and Supplementary Benefit) Regulations 1977 (SI 1977 No 674)

Income Support (General) Regulations 1987 (SI 1987 No 1967)

Industrial Relations Act 1971

Rehabilitation of Offenders Act 1974

Rehabilitation of Offenders Act 1974 (Exceptions) Order 1975 (SI 1975 No 1023)

Rehabilitation of Offenders Act 1974 (Exceptions) (Amendment) Orders 1986 (SI 1986 No 1249 and SI 1986 No 2268)

Sex Discrimination Act 1986

Social Security (Unemployment, Sickness and Invalidity Benefit) Regulations 1983 (SI 1983 No 1598)

Transfer of Undertakings (Protection of Employment) Regulations 1981 (SI 1981 No 1794)

TABLE OF CASES

LIST OF ABBREVIATIONS

AC	Appeal Cases
ACAS	Advisory, Conciliation and Arbitration Service
ALL ER	All England Reports
CA	Court of Appeal
COIT	Central Office of Industrial Tribunals
DSS	Department of Social Security
EAT	Employment Appeal Tribunal
EC	European Community
ECJ	European Court of Justice
EDT	Effective date of termination
EPCA	Employment Protection (Consolidation) Act 1978
ETO	Economic, technical or organisational
HL	House of Lords
ICR	Industrial Cases Reports
ILJ	Industrial Law Journal
IRLR	Industrial Relations Law Report
ITR	Industrial Tribunal Reports
MSC	Manpower Services Commission
NALGO	National and Local Government Officers' Association
NIRC	National Industrial Relations Court
QB	Queen's Bench
s	section
sch	schedule

PREFACE

The purpose of this book is to provide employers, employees, trade union officials and personnel officers with straightforward and practical guidance on the case law and statutes which make up the substantive law of unfair dismissal. The book offers an up to date analysis of the law, while giving particular attention to commonly recurring disciplinary issues and how these matters should be handled. This book does not attempt to deal with the rules of procedure which govern the action of unfair dismissal, but concerns itself solely with the substantive law. Those readers who wish to develop a practical understanding of tribunal procedures are referred to this book's 'stablemate' in the Employment Law Guide series, *Industrial Tribunals – How to Present Your Case* by Philip Parry.

Employment law is a dynamic area and writing an up to date guide to unfair dismissal is akin to trying to hit a rapidly moving target. I have, however, tried to cover developments in the case law up to and including 1 May 1991.

1 INTRODUCTION

The right to claim unfair dismissal has been part of the legal framework of employment relations since 28 February 1972, when it was introduced as part of the now repealed Industrial Relations Act 1971. It was introduced because the common law did not provide adequate protection against arbitrary terminations of employment and also in an attempt to reduce the number of strikes over dismissals.

The weakness of protection against dismissal under the common law

At common law a contract of employment can be lawfully terminated simply by giving notice, the length of such notice having been expressly agreed. In the absence of an expressed notice period, the common law implies a period of 'reasonable notice' whose length will depend on the circumstances of the employment. Moreover, the common law allows an employer to dismiss an employee with no notice at all if the latter's conduct amounted to a repudiation of the contract of employment.

So until the introduction of the statutory right to claim unfair dismissal, the employer possessed an extremely wide power in the area of discipline, given the largely obsolete and unjust legal principles which constituted the common law action of wrongful dismissal. The major weaknesses, from the employee's point of view, in the action for wrongful dismissal can be summarised as follows:

- The general failure of the common law action to question the fairness of the employer's decision to terminate the contract, allowing an employer to dismiss for any reason – however arbitrary – provided the correct period of notice was given.
- The low level of damages awarded to successful litigants, generally only compensating for the appropriate notice period which should have been given.
- The inability of the dismissed employee to regain his or her job because of the traditional reluctance of the courts to order reinstatement of the employee.

- The archaic nature of some of the principles of summary dismissal reflecting 'almost an attitude of Tsar–serf' (as Lord Justice Edmund Davies put it in **Wilson v M Racher**).
- The lack of procedural protections for most employees, with only an ill-defined group of so-called 'office-holders' being entitled to natural justice, including the right to state their case before dismissal.

With the advent of statutory unfair dismissal, the common law action was perceived as largely irrelevant in practical terms. After all, the statutory remedy *was* concerned with the overall merits of the employer's decision to dismiss, and the determination of the fairness of the dismissal also involved a scrutiny of the procedure adopted by the employer in taking disciplinary action. Moreover, it did provide for reinstatement or re-engagement as remedies.

The impact of the right to claim unfair dismissal

The right to claim unfair dismissal is undoubtedly the most significant of the employment rights which were introduced during the 1970s. In quantitative terms, unfair dismissal claims dominate the work of industrial tribunals, accounting for around 70 per cent of their workload. In addition, the introduction of the claim produced significant changes in employment relations practices during the 1970s, encouraging the reform or formalisation of procedures adopted by employers in taking disciplinary action.

The significance of this particular employment right is further enhanced because it is popularly portrayed as a powerful, perhaps too powerful, constraint on managerial prerogative. Indeed, there is a potent mythology among sections of British managers that holds that the law relating to unfair dismissal makes it almost impossible to dismiss even the most deserving case. This view persists in the face of judicial decisions, research and statistics which raise questions as to the extent to which the legislative code on unfair dismissal does effectively control management's power of discipline.

By the 1980s, commentators had identified the following short-comings in the action for unfair dismissal:

1   The generally low success rate of applicants. (The term 'applicant' or 'complainant' refers to the party bringing a claim before an industrial tribunal. The party answering the claim is known as the 'respondent'.) In 1988–9, 17,870 cases were disposed of (this figure represents a steady decline in unfair dismissal applications over recent years). Of these, 11,814 (66 per cent) were settled without a hearing, either by ACAS conciliated settlement (6,935) or by some other form of withdrawal (4,879). Of the 5,786 cases actually heard by industrial tribunals, 3,620 were dismissed and 2,166 were upheld, a success rate for employee applicants of 37.5 per cent (in 1981 this had reached a low of 23 per cent).

2   The few cases in which the reinstatement remedy is awarded. Of the cases upheld in 1988-9 only 58 ended in an order for reinstatement and re-engagement (2.7 per cent of successful claims; 1 per cent of cases heard; 0.32 per cent of cases disposed of).

3   The low level of compensation. Of the cases upheld by industrial tribunals in 1988–9 which resulted in compensation, the median award was £1,732 – an actual fall on the previous year's median award of £1,865 (statistical source: *Employment Gazette*, April 1990 pages 213–18).

4   The devaluation between 1979 and 1987 of the importance of adhering to fair procedures in unfair dismissal as a result of the application of the test laid down in ***British Labour Pump Co Ltd*** v ***Byrne*** (now no longer good law as a result of the Law Lords' decision in ***Polkey*** v ***AE Dayton Services Ltd.***

Revived interest in wrongful dismissal

It is ironic that, given these flaws in the framework of statutory protection, there has been a renewed interest in common law remedies by employees who are seeking to prevent a dismissal from taking place in breach of a contractually binding disciplinary procedure, or to restrain some other breach of contract by the employer. The judicial response has been to show less reluctance in granting injunctions to prevent such breaches taking place.

The decision in *Irani v Southampton and South West Hampshire Health Authority* is a good example of this development. The plaintiff was an ophthalmologist who was employed part-time in an out patient eye clinic. He was dismissed with six weeks' notice because of irreconcilable differences with the consultant in charge of the clinic. No criticism at all was made of his competence or conduct.

In dismissing Mr Irani the employers were in breach of the disciplinary procedure established by the Whitley Council and incorporated in his contract of employment. He sought an injunction to prevent the employers from dismissing him without first following the appropriate disciplinary procedure. The employers argued that this would be contrary to the general rule that injunctions cannot be issued to keep a contract of employment alive. The plaintiff obtained his injunction.

The judge ruled that the case fell within the exception to the general rule for the following reasons. First, trust and confidence remained between employer and employee. The Health Authority retained complete faith in the honesty, integrity and loyalty of Mr Irani; any breakdown in confidence was between the consultant and Mr Irani, not Mr Irani and the Authority. Second, damages would not be an adequate remedy, since Mr Irani would become virtually unemployable throughout the National Health Service and would lose the right to use NHS facilities to treat his private patients.

The case law on the use of injunctions to restrain dismissals and other breaches of contract is in a state of flux. *Irani* and other cases where this remedy has been obtained have been somewhat unusual because the court was satisfied on the facts that the integrity and ability of the employee were not in question. In the more usual disciplinary case, the court will more readily accept that trust and confidence have been destroyed and refuse to grant the order. Fortunately, the House of Lords' reassertion of the importance of procedural fairness in *Polkey*, has now restored a degree of potency to unfair dismissal action which had been sadly lacking for some time and, for most employees, it remains the most effective remedy. But a wrongful dismissal claim is worth considering where:

- the employee is a high earner whose losses in terms of salary and fringe benefits far exceed the relatively low maximum compensation limits set for unfair dismissal

- the employee is prevented from claiming unfair dismissal because he or she lacks sufficient continuity of service, is over retirement age or has failed to lodge a complaint within three months
- the dismissal is in breach of contract and the employee wishes to seek an injunction to keep the contract alive.

Excessive legalism

In the decade or so since the introduction of the right to claim unfair dismissal, the amount of case law has burgeoned and so has its complexity. As early as 1975 the first President of the Employment Appeal Tribunal (EAT), Phillips J, was moved to remark 'The expression unfair dismissal is in no sense a common sense expression capable of being understood by the man in the street' (*W Devis & Sons Ltd* v *Atkins*).

So, while the industrial tribunals and the procedure under which they operate were designed to provide a speedy, cheap and informal mechanism for the resolution of disputes over dismissal, the law they have to apply is often of great complexity. It is, therefore, not surprising that just over one-third of applicants and over one-half of respondent employers are legally represented at tribunal hearings (see *Patterns of representation of the parties in unfair dismissal cases: a review of the evidence* by WR Hawes and G Smith, DE Research Paper No 22 (1981)).

This tendency towards excessive legalism has been recognised by the Court of Appeal, and in a series of rulings it has adopted a two-pronged strategy designed to reverse the trend and reduce the number of cases coming through on appeal from industrial tribunals to the EAT.

First, it has ruled that many issues in employment law are ultimately questions of fact and not questions of law. Given that appeal to the EAT *must* involve a claim that the industrial tribunal misdirected itself in law, this is clearly an attempt to return decision making to the tribunals. The following are examples of this policy of classifying issues as questions of fact and thus limiting the possibility of appeals:

- whether a worker is an 'employee'
- whether a 'constructive dismissal' has taken place

- whether an employee resigned or was forced to do so
- whether it was reasonably practicable to present an unfair dismissal claim on time.

The second element of the strategy against legalism has been the Court of Appeal's rejection of the EAT's practice of laying down guidelines for tribunals to follow when confronted with major problem areas of unfair dismissal law, eg redundancy procedure, suspected dishonesty, long-term sickness absence. The nature of the Court of Appeal's attack on what was seen as the EAT's unduly interventionist role is clearly illustrated by the following statement of Lord Justice Lawton in *Bailey* v *BP Oil (Kent Refinery) Ltd*:

'Each case must depend on its own facts. In our judgement it is unwise for this court or the Employment Appeal Tribunal to set out guidelines, and wrong to make rules and establish presumptions for industrial tribunals to follow or take into account.'

While the concern of the Court of Appeal to rid the law of unfair dismissal of excessive legal technicality is understandable, it may be that the Court has taken matters too far and that the attack on legalism and the proliferation of appeals may be achieved at the cost of certainty and consistency. In the absence of established guidelines and precedent, it becomes extremely difficult for legal or personnel practitioners to offer advice on any particular case. For example, if the question of 'employee' status is classified a question of fact, there is every prospect that industrial tribunals in different parts of the country can come to diametrically opposed conclusions in cases involving identical facts, and with little or no prospect of the EAT resolving the matter on appeal.

Nevertheless, a decade or so of unfair dismissal law has produced a comprehensive body of case law which offers valuable guidance and which is often applied. It is an analysis of those decisions and the legislation which together comprise the law of unfair dismissal to which we now turn our attention.

Where to find the law

Over the last 18 years or so, the legislation governing unfair dismissal has remained largely unaltered — the major amendments being concerned with dismissal for non-union membership. The other significant change concerned the qualification period necessary to claim, which was raised from 26 weeks in 1979 to the current level of two years in 1985.

In 1978, an attempt was made to consolidate the legislation in the Employment Protection (Consolidation) Act, and ss54—80 still contain the relevant provisions. Since 1978, however, a number of amendments have been made via a succession of Employment Acts, the Sex Discrimination Act 1986 and a number of pieces of delegated legislation.

In the ensuing chapters, the Employment Protection (Consolidation) Act 1978 (as amended) will be referred to as EPCA.

Key stages in the law

For analytical purposes the law of unfair dismissal may be divided into four parts or stages (see page 8).

Stage 1 — Has a dismissal taken place?

The three forms of statutory dismissal:

- direct dismissal
- lapse of a fixed-term contract
- constructive dismissal.

will be discussed in the next chapter. If there is a dispute on whether dismissal has taken place, the burden of proof is on the employee.

UNFAIR DISMISSAL

The four stages of unfair dismissal

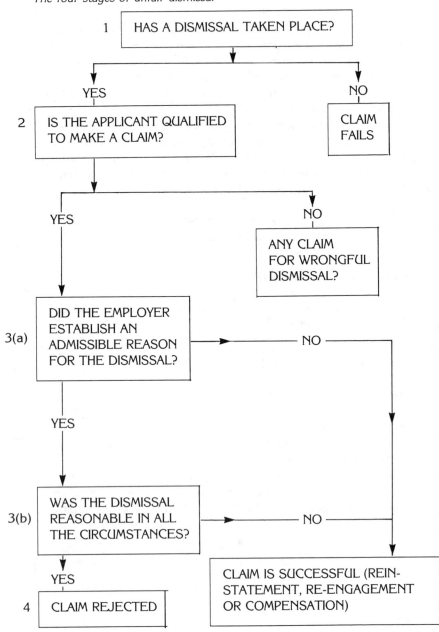

Stage 2 – Is the applicant qualified to make a claim?

The tribunal must be satisfied on three issues, namely:

- that the applicant is an 'employee'
- that the applicant's employment does not fall within an excluded category *and*
- that the applicant has presented the complaint in time.

Stage 3 – Is the dismissal fair or unfair?

This stage involves the tribunals producing answers to two broad questions:

- has the employer established that the reason or principal reason for the dismissal was an 'admissible' reason? *and*
- in the circumstances did the employer act reasonably in treating it as a sufficient reason for dismissing the employee?

Stage 4 – Remedies

Once the tribunal is satisfied that an employee has been unfairly dismissed, it has to consider one of three forms of remedy:

- an order for reinstatement
- an order of re-engagement
- an award of compensation (see EPCA ss67–9).

2 THE CONCEPT OF DISMISSAL

The common law action of wrongful dismissal and the statutory rights to claim unfair dismissal and redundancy payments all depend on a dismissal taking place. If the employer can successfully argue that the job ended in a way which was *not* a dismissal, then the industrial tribunal will not even go on to consider the merits of his or her actions and liability is avoided. The variety of ways the contract of employment can come to an end in legal terms include:

1   Termination not involving dismissal:
    * death or dissolution of the employer
    * frustration
    * expiry of fixed term contracts
    * mutual agreement.

2   Termination involving dismissal at common law:
    * dismissal by notice
    * dismissal for fundamental breach of contract
    * wrongful dismissal.

3   Termination deemed to be dismissal by EPCA:
    * an act of the employer or an event affecting the employer (including death, dissolution of a partnership, or winding up of a company) which has the effect of terminating the contract automatically at common law, will be deemed to be a dismissal for the purposes of redundancy but *not* for an unfair dismissal claim (EPCA s93)
    * termination of the contract by the employer with or without notice (EPCA ss55(2)(a) and 83(2)(a))
    * the failure to renew a fixed-term contract (EPCA ss55(2)(b) and 83(2)(b))
    * where the employee terminates the contract, with or without notice, in circumstances such that he or she is entitled to terminate it without notice by reason of the employer's conduct: 'constructive dismissal' (EPCA ss55(2)(c) and 83(2)(c)).

Terminations which may not amount to dismissal

Frustration

'Frustration' is a legal concept which, if it applies, brings the employment contract *automatically* to an end. As a result, the employer does not have to go on paying wages, or pay compensation for unfair dismissal, redundancy, etc.

In order for frustration to apply, there are two essential factors which must be present:

1   There must be some event, not foreseen or provided for by the parties to the contract, which either makes it *impossible for the contract to be performed at all*, or at least renders its performance something *radically different from what the parties envisaged when they made the contract* and

2   The event must have occurred without the fault of either contracting party. Frustration will not operate if it was 'self-induced' or caused by the fault of a party.

Events which have been held to frustrate the contract include the following:

• the conscription of the employee to national service
• internment as an enemy alien during wartime.

However, frustration arguments have been most frequently employed in the cases of long-term absence through sickness or through imprisonment.

Sickness

In relation to sickness absence, a number of principles will be relevant in deciding whether a contract is frustrated. In **Williams v Watson's Luxury Coaches Ltd**, the EAT usefully summarised the relevant principles in deciding whether a contract is frustrated through sickness as follows:

- the court must guard against too easy an application of the doctrine, more especially when redundancy occurs and also when the true situation may be dismissal by redundancy
- although it is not necessary to decide that frustration occurred on a particular date, nevertheless an attempt to decide the relevant date is a far from useless exercise, as it may help to determine in the mind of the court whether it is a true frustration situation
- there are a number of factors which may help decide the issue including:
  - the length of the previous employment
  - how long it had been expected the employment would continue
  - the nature of the job
  - the nature, length and effect of the illness or disabling event
  - the need of the employer for the work to be done
  - the need for a replacement to do it
  - the risk of the employer acquiring obligations in respect of redundancy payments to the person who has replaced the absent employee
  - whether wages have continued to be paid
  - the actions and statements of the employer, particularly whether the employer has sought to dismiss the sick employee
  - whether it is reasonable, in all the circumstances, to expect the employer to keep the job open any longer.
- the party alleging the frustration should not be allowed to rely on the frustrating event if that event was caused by the fault of that party.

The case of *Notcutt* v *Universal Equipment Co London Ltd* provides a good illustration of the operation of the frustration doctrine. Mr Notcutt had been employed by the same relatively small company as a skilled workman for some 27 years. In October 1983, when two years from retirement age, he suffered a coronary and was thereafter off work. His employers sub-contracted his work on a temporary basis, but this was not wholly satisfactory, and by July 1984 decided to take on someone else if Mr Notcutt was not going to return to work. With Mr Notcutt's permission, the employers sought a medical report from his general practitioner. In that report, the doctor said that he doubted whether Mr Notcutt would ever work again. As a result Mr Notcutt was given 12 weeks' notice of dismissal.

Mr Notcutt took legal advice and was informed correctly that under EPCA he was entitled to sick pay during the notice period, notwithstanding that ordinarily under his contract he was not paid when off sick. He lodged a claim to that effect in the county court.

Ultimately, the Court of Appeal decided that the county court judge was correct in finding that Mr Notcutt's contract of employment had been frustrated by an illness which would have probably prevented him from working again. The contract, therefore, was not terminated by the employers and Mr Notcutt *was not* entitled to sick pay during the notice period.

Imprisonment

In the past, imprisonment was thought to be 'self-induced' frustration. More recently, however, the Court of Appeal has ruled that a custodial sentence of six months *did* have the effect of frustrating a four year apprenticeship contract which still had 24 months to run. It was felt that it was the sentence passed by the trial judge – as opposed to the employee's criminal conduct – which was the frustrating event. Consequently, this was not a case of self-induced frustration (*FC Shepherd & Co Ltd* v *Jerrom*).

The courts have provided very little guidance as to how long a sentence of imprisonment has to be in order to frustrate the contract. In *Harrington* v *Kent County Council*, a sentence of 12 months' imprisonment was found to have frustrated the contract, even though the sentence was later quashed on appeal.

In *Chakki* v *United East Co Ltd*, the EAT was of the view that in imprisonment cases, whether or not frustration had occurred could be determined by answering the following questions:

'1   Looking at the matter from a practical commercial point of view, when was it necessary for the employers to decide as to the employee's future and as to whether a replacement ... would have to be engaged?   2   At the time when the decision had to be taken, what would a reasonable employer have considered to be the likely length of the employee's absence over the next few months?   3   If in the light of his likely absence it appeared necessary to engage a replacement, was it reasonable to engage a permanent replacement rather than a temporary one?'

While frustration arguments may well succeed in exceptional cases, the courts are generally reluctant to apply the doctrine. In **Williams v Watson's Luxury Coaches Ltd** (above), the EAT attributed this judicial caution to the view that the doctrine can do harm to good industrial relations, as it provides an easy escape from the obligations of investigation which should be carried out by a reasonable employer. It is therefore better for the employer to take dismissal action. Advice on how dismissals for long-term sickness should be handled is offered in chapter 6.

Fixed-term and 'task' contracts

The expiry of a fixed-term contract is regarded as a dismissal. Such a contract must have a definite starting and finishing date, although there may be provision for earlier termination by notice within the fixed-term period (**BBC v Dixon**). This protection offered to those on fixed-term contracts represents a limited recognition on the part of those who drafted the legislation that any other approach would invite employers to employ large sections of their workforce under such arrangements and so avoid liability for unfair dismissal and redundancy payments.

However, this protection is very limited for two reasons. First, a dismissal of an employee who comes to the end of a 'temporary' contract may, in the circumstances, be held to be fair as 'some other substantial reason' (see later). Second, EPCA s142 states that where an employee is employed for a fixed-term of a year or more he or she may agree in writing to exclude any right he or she may have to claim unfair dismissal, and if employed for two years to exclude any right to claim redundancy payments also, should the contract not be renewed at the completion of its term.

Moreover, the courts have made a distinction between a fixed-term contract, deemed to be a dismissal under the legislation, and a contract for the completion of a particular task, at the end of which there is no dismissal. A 'task' contract is discharged by performance of the particular task and cannot give rise to a dismissal, eg a seaman engaged for a particular voyage or a person hired to paint a house.

In **Brown v Knowsley Borough Council**, the distinction between a fixed-term contract and a contract to perform a particular task was extended to cover contracts terminable on the happening or non-happening of a future event. In this case, a further education college lecturer, having been previously employed under a number of fixed-term contracts, was then employed under a one year temporary contract from 1 September 1983, which was expressed to last only so long as sufficient funds were provided by the Manpower Services Commission to support the course she taught. On 3 August 1984, she was given written notice that, as MSC funds had ceased to be available, her employment would terminate on 31 August 1984. The applicant's claim for a redundancy payment was rejected by the industrial tribunal and the EAT on the basis that there had been no dismissal, and that her contract was terminable on the happening or non-happening of a future event, ie the withdrawal of MSC sponsorship.

Termination by mutual agreement

As with other contracts, a contract of employment may be terminated by the mutual consent of the parties. If the courts were to accept too readily that the contractual relationship had ended in this way then access to employment protection would be severely threatened. As a result, statute has intervened by providing that:

> 'where an employee under notice gives the employer notice that s/he wishes to leave before the expiry of the employers' notice, the employee is deemed still to have been dismissed for unfair dismissal and redundancy purposes and not party to a early termination by mutual consent.' (EPCA ss55(3), 85(2))

In general, the courts and tribunals have been reluctant to accept the argument that an employee has in reality agreed to give up their job and forego the possibility of an unfair dismissal or redundancy claim.

In *Igbo* v *Johnson Matthey Chemicals Ltd*, the Court of Appeal had to consider the effect of an agreement by which an employee agrees that if he or she does not return to work from a period of extended leave by a specified time, then the contract of employment will come to an end. In overruling the earlier decision in *British Leyland (UK) Ltd* v *Ashraf*, the Court of Appeal held that these 'automatic termination' agreements were void under EPCA s140. This section makes void any provision in an agreement which purports to 'exclude or limit' any provision of EPCA. By limiting Ms Igbo's right to claim unfair dismissal, the agreement offended s140(1). Dismissals for overstaying leave, therefore, must be subject to the test of reasonableness and the ACAS Advisory Handbook, *Discipline At Work* (page 42), provides guidance on how such matters should be handled.

A factor which weighed heavily with the Court of Appeal in *Igbo* was that, if such 'automatic termination' were allowed, then there would be nothing to prevent an employer including a term in the contract stating that if the employee was more than five minutes late for work on any day, for whatever reason, the contract would automatically come to an end. In this way, the protection offered by the unfair dismissal legislation would be non-existent.

For similar policy reasons to those described above, the courts have held that a resignation under threat of dismissal may constitute a dismissal (see *Sheffield* v *Oxford Controls Co Ltd*).

The distinction between a mutual termination on acceptable terms and a forced resignation was crucial to the EAT's decision in *Logan Salton* v *Durham County Council*. Mr Logan Salton was employed by the local authority as a social worker. The local authority commenced disciplinary proceedings against him, based on a report from the director of social services which recommended that he should be summarily dismissed. With the assistance of NALGO he negotiated a severance payment which repaid an outstanding council car loan of £2,750 and signed a written agreement with the local authority that his contract of employment would terminate by 'mutual agreement'. Mr Logan Salton then claimed that he had been unfairly dismissed and that the mutual agreement to terminate was either void as an agreement entered into under duress, or void because it contravened s140.

The EAT upheld the industrial tribunal's decision that there had been no dismissal in law. The present case was distinguishable on its facts from that of *Igbo* v *Johnson Matthey Chemicals Ltd* (above), relied upon by the appellant. The agreement between the appellant and the respondent was not a contract of employment or a variation of an existing contract. It was a separate contract which was entered into willingly, without duress, after proper advice and for a financial inducement. Therefore the agreement was not caught by s140.

So it is not the case that an argument based upon termination by mutual consent can never succeed, for example, where a termination is willingly agreed to by the employee in return for financial compensation, as in *Salton* itself, or under an early retirement scheme, as in *University of Liverpool* v *Humber*.

Constructive resignation

In a number of cases in the 1970s, the EAT was prepared to accept that certain acts of gross misconduct by an employee *automatically* terminated the contract without the need for the employer to dismiss. A good example of what was known as 'self-dismissal' or 'constructive resignation' is *Gannon* v *JC Firth Ltd*, where employees 'downed tools' and walked out of the factory, leaving machinery in a dangerous state. They did not let the company know they were leaving and did not return to work the next day. It was held that they had dismissed themselves by their actions.

Following the Court of Appeal's judgement in *London Transport Executive* v *Clarke*, it is clear that 'self-dismissal' arguments will no longer be successful. In this case, the majority of the Court of Appeal held that a contract of employment could not be 'automatically' terminated by a serious breach of contract on the part of the employee – the terminating event was the *dismissal* by the employer in response to that serious breach.

Statutory dismissals

The EPCA has extended the concept of dismissal beyond termination by the employer with or without notice, to cover the non-renewal of a fixed-term contract and cases of 'constructive dismissal'. What constitutes a fixed-term contract has already been examined and below, some of the issues which have arisen in relation to the two other forms of dismissal – direct and constructive dismissal – are discussed.

Direct dismissal (EPCA s55(2)(a))

This is the clearest and most obvious form of dismissal where unequivocal words of termination are used and a date of termination set. Consequently, the concept has not generated a significant amount of case law. Nevertheless, the following issues have arisen:

'Resign or be sacked'

A resignation under threat of dismissal may constitute a dismissal (see *East Sussex County Council* v *Walker* and *Sheffield* v *Oxford Controls Co Ltd*). However, in order to succeed in this argument the employee must establish a certain and immediate threat (*Martin* v *Glynwed Distribution Ltd*).

Ambiguous/unambiguous words of dismissal/resignation

One problem which occasionally arises in dismissal cases is whether or not the words used by the employer amount to a dismissal, eg they may have been merely intended as a rebuke or uttered in the heat of the moment. The problem can also arise in the reverse, where the employee uses words which the employer chooses to interpret as a resignation.

The legal principles in this area may be summarised as follows:

1   If, *taking into account the context in which they were uttered*, the words unambiguously amount to a dismissal (or resignation) then this should be the finding of the tribunal.

For example, when Mrs Southern, an office manager in a firm of solicitors, announced to the partners at the end of a partners' meeting 'I am resigning', the Court of Appeal held her to her unambiguous statement (*Southern* v *Franks Charlesly & Co*).

2   Where, however, the words used are ambiguous, perhaps because they were uttered in the heat of the moment, the effect of the statement is determined by an objective test, ie whether any 'reasonable' employer or employee might have understood the words to be tantamount to a dismissal or resignation.

A rather colourful example is provided by *Futty* v *D and D Brekkes Ltd*. Futty was a fish filleter on Hull dock. During an altercation with his foreman, Futty was told, 'If you do not like the job, fuck off'. Futty stated that he interpreted the foreman's words as words of dismissal; the company denied dismissing him. The industrial tribunal heard evidence from other fish filleters as to the meaning they would give to the words used because it was important to interpret the words 'not in isolation — but against the background of the fishdock'. The fish filleters, who had witnessed the incident, did not consider that Futty had been dismissed, and the industrial tribunal agreed, stating that 'once the question of dismissal becomes imminent bad language tends to disappear and an unexpected formality seems to descend on the parties'. Futty was held to have terminated his own employment.

3 A dismissal or resignation given in the heat of the moment may be withdrawn. However, it is probable that retraction must follow almost immediately.

Once notice of resignation or dismissal is given, it cannot be retracted without the consent of the other party to the contract. It may be that one exception to this general rule is where the words of dismissal or resignation uttered in the heat of the moment may be withdrawn, provided the retraction follows almost immediately (see *Martin* v *Yeomen Aggregates Ltd*).

Constructive dismissal (EPCA s55(2)(C))

The problems surrounding this form of dismissal have generated a mass of case law over the years. By virtue of the concept of constructive dismissal, the law treats some resignations as dismissals and therefore extends statutory dismissal rights to those employees who are forced to resign by virtue of their employer's conduct. This form of dismissal may be extremely important in the context of reorganisations, where employers may be seeking to introduce changes in terms and conditions of employment.

Under the current definition, which applies to both unfair and redundancy dismissals, it does not matter whether the employee left with or without notice, provided he or she was entitled to leave by reason of the employer's conduct.

In the mid 1970s there was a difference of opinion among the judiciary as to the criteria which should be used in order to determine whether a constructive dismissal had taken place. Specifically, a number of decisions suggested that constructive dismissal was not confined, as had been previously assumed, to fundamental breaches of contract, but applied to any case where the employer's behaviour was held to be unreasonable.

Following a period of confusion, the Court of Appeal in *Western*

Excavating (ECC) Ltd v *Sharp* clarified matters, rejecting the reasonableness test, and holding that a contractual approach was the right one.

The key elements of the concept are as follows:

- Has the employer broken a term of the contract or made it clear that he or she does not intend to be bound by the contract?
- If yes, is the term which has or will be broken an essential or fundamental term of the contract?
- If yes, has the employee resigned with or without notice in response to the breach within a reasonable time?

What constitutes a breach of a fundamental term and how long is a reasonable time? The difficulty in knowing where the employer or employee stands on these and other issues has been compounded by a development which has been referred to in the previous chapter. This is the recent tendency of the Court of Appeal to hold that many of the issues in unfair dismissal, most notably the question as to whether there has been a serious breach of contract, are issues of fact alone or mixed fact and law. Therefore, the findings of industrial tribunals are only reviewable following perverse decisions (*Pedersen* v *Camden London Borough Council* and *Woods* v *WM Car Services*).

In the midst of this uncertainty, however, it is possible to produce a two part categorisation of acts or omissions which have been held to repudiate the contract by the courts and tribunals:

1 An employer may break a positive contractual obligation to the employee, eg withdrawal of free transport or failure to pay wages.

2 The employer may insist that the employee agree to a change in existing working arrangements or terms and conditions of employment, eg a change of shift, or insist that the employee perform duties which he or she is not obliged under the contract to carry out.

Following the adoption of the contractual test by the Court of Appeal in *Western Excavating* (above), a number of commentators argued that it would impose a great restriction on the scope of constructive dismissal claims relative to the more generous reasonableness test. This has not occurred because the EAT has been prepared to hold that *contracts of employment generally are subject to an implied term that the employer must not destroy or seriously damage the relationship of trust and confidence between employer and employee.* As a result, the difference between the **Western Excavating** approach and the discredited 'reasonableness' test looks rather slight, as is illustrated by looking at some of the situations where the implied obligation has been held to be broken:

- failure to respond to an employee's complaints about the lack of adequate safety equipment (**British Aircraft Corporation Ltd v Austin**)
- undermining of the authority of senior staff over subordinates (**Courtaulds Northern Textiles Ltd v Andrew**)
- failure to provide an employee with reasonable support to enable him or her to carry out work without disruption and harassment from fellow employees (**Wigan Borough Council v Davies**)
- failure to properly investigate allegations of sexual harassment or to treat the complaint with sufficient seriousness (**Bracebridge Engineering Ltd v Darby**)
- foul language by employer (**Palmanor Ltd v Cedron**)
- imposition of a disciplinary penalty grossly out of proportion to the offence (**BBC v Beckett**)
- a series of minor incidents of harassment over a period of time which cumulatively amount to repudiation – the so-called 'last straw' doctrine (**Woods v WM Car Services** (above)).

The potency of the implied obligation of trust and confidence can be seen in the case of **United Bank Ltd v Akhtar**, which suggests that even where the contract contains a wide mobility clause, employers must still operate the clause in a reasonable manner. Should they fail to do so, it may constitute a breach of contract and entitle the employee to claim constructive dismissal.

Mr Akhtar was a junior ranking and low paid employee who had worked for the bank in Leeds since 1978. A clause in his contract provided:

'The Bank may from time to time require an employee to be transferred temporarily or permanently to any place of business which the Bank may have in the UK for which a location or other allowance may be payable at the discretion of the Bank.'

The EAT held that the employee was entitled to treat himself as constructively dismissed by reason of the employer's conduct in requiring him to transfer his place of employment from Leeds to Birmingham at short notice (six days) and with no financial assistance, even if it could be held within the terms of the express mobility clause in the employee's contract of employment. This is because the general implied contractual duty set out in **Woods v WM Car Services** (above) is that employers will not, without reasonable and proper cause, conduct themselves in a manner calculated or likely to destroy the relationship of trust and confidence between employer and employee. This is an overriding obligation independent of, and in addition to, the literal terms of the contract.

Fairness and constructive dismissal

A constructive dismissal is not necessarily an unfair dismissal. Tribunals, having first determined whether the elements of constructive dismissal are present, will then go on to consider the fairness question under EPCA s57(3). In many cases, this will not alter their conclusion, but there may be cases such as those concerned with business reorganisations where, although the employee was entitled to resign, the employer's action which prompted the resignation is held to be fair and reasonable in the circumstances.

In **Savoia v Chiltern Herb Farms Ltd**, the employers embarked on a reorganisation of duties after the death of one of their foremen. They decided to move Mr Savoia from his role as supervisor in the packing department, following complaints about his performance, and to offer him the dead man's former position – that of foreman in charge of the production department.

Despite the offer of a higher salary, Mr Savoia refused to move to the new post because he was concerned that he would be exposed to conjunctivitis as a result of the heat and smoke in the production department. He refused the employer's offer of a medical examination so that they could judge whether his concerns were well-founded.

Both the industrial tribunal and the EAT found that he had been constructively dismissed, but that the dismissal was for 'some other substantial reason', and fair. The Court of Appeal upheld the decision on the basis that 'the reorganisation of the business was imperative', and Mr Savoia's 'refusal to be medically examined when he protested that production work was unsuitable for him created a situation which was a substantial reason' for the dismissal, and fair.

3 IS THE APPLICANT QUALIFIED TO MAKE A CLAIM?

In order to make a claim for unfair dismissal, the applicant must satisfy the industrial tribunal on the following broad issues:

1 That the applicant is an 'employee'.

2 That the applicant's employment does not fall within an excluded category.

3 That the applicant has presented the claim in time.

Employee status

The distinction between contracts of employment and self-employment is of fundamental importance. Only 'employees' qualify for employment protection rights such as unfair dismissal, redundancy payments, minimum notice on termination, etc. It is, therefore, unfortunate that the formulation of the test of employee status has come from the courts and tribunals rather than from statute. The only guidance on the question in the legislation is so completely circular as to be absolutely useless (see EPCA s153).

The case law on this subject is confusing and contradictory. Historically, the leading approach was to apply the test of 'control', ie could the employer control how, when and where the person was to work — if so, that person was his or her employee. However, as nowadays many employees possess skills not held by their employer, control as the sole determinant of status was rejected. Along the way the test of 'integration' was floated, ie whether the person was fully integrated into the employing organisation, but this test was never widely adopted.

The modern approach has been to abandon the search for a single test and adopt a test which weighs up all the factors for and against the existence of a contract of employment to determine whether the person was 'in business on his own account' (see *Ready Mixed Concrete (South East) Ltd* v *Minister of Pensions and National Insurance* and *Market Investigations* v *Minister of Social Security*).

The judgement of Mr Justice Cooke in the *Market Investigations* decision offers the following checklist for employment status:

'No exhaustive list can be compiled of the considerations which are relevant to [the] question, nor can strict rules be laid down as to the relevant weight which the various considerations should carry in particular cases. The most that can be said is that control will no doubt always have to be considered, although it can no longer be regarded as the sole determining factor; and that factors which may be of importance are such matters as whether the man performing the services provides his own equipment, whether he hires his own helpers, what degree of financial risk he takes, what degree of responsibility for investment and management he has, and whether and how far he has an opportunity of profiting from the sound management of his task.' (page 185)

The business test, together with the checklist set out above, received the approval of the Privy Council in *Lee* v *Chung and Shun Sing Construction and Engineering Co Ltd.*

Recent case law involving the question of the status of temporary and casual workers has seen an emphasis placed on the concept of mutuality of obligation as a possible factor in the equation. This was explained by Lord Justice Kerr in *Nethermere (St Neots) Ltd* v *Gardiner and Taverna* as follows:

'The inescapable requirement concerning the alleged employees, however, is that they must be subject to an obligation to accept and perform some minimum, or at least reasonable, amount of work for the alleged employer.'

The implications of this test for people with irregular working patterns are highly disadvantageous — at least if it is applied in a strict sense. The dangers are highlighted in the case of *O'Kelly* v

Trusthouse Forte plc. In this case, the Court of Appeal was not prepared to find that 'regular' casual waiters were employees, even though they had a well-established and regular working relationship with Trusthouse Forte. It was held to be quite 'unreal' to maintain that the long-standing arrangement, which involved a reliance by the employer on its regular casuals and of the regulars receiving priority in the allocation of work, had the essential 'mutuality of obligation' to classify them as employees. Mutuality was lacking because technically they could refuse work when it was offered even though, in practice, they did not do so because refusal would result in removal from the regular casual list.

This sort of narrow reasoning is also to be found in the judgement of the EAT in *Wickens* **v** *Champion Employment* where 'temps' engaged by a private employment agency were not accorded employment status. This was because of the lack of binding obligation on the part of the agency to make bookings for work and the absence of any obligation by the temps to accept them.

A more liberal approach is to be found in the majority judgements of the Court of Appeal in the *Nethermere* case. Here, homeworkers making clothing on a piecework basis were accorded employee status on the grounds that the regular giving and taking of work over a period of time evidenced the necessary mutuality of obligation. This was so even though the homeworkers were under no obligation to undertake a particular quantity of work, and in certain weeks did no work at all. As Lord Justice Stephenson put it:

> 'I cannot see why well-founded expectations of continuing homework should not be hardened or refined into enforceable contracts by regular giving and taking of work over periods of a year or more, and why outworkers should not thereby become employees under contracts of service . . .'

The confusions which abound in this area are multiplied because of the view that the question of employment status is one of mixed fact and law rather than a pure question of law (see *O'Kelly* **v** *Trusthouse Forte plc* (above). As a result, the powers of the EAT and Court of Appeal to interfere with decisions of industrial tribunals on status are much reduced, and the chances of inconsistency thereby heightened. Those who regretted the adoption of this view, welcomed the House of Lords' decision in **Davies v Presbyterian Church of Wales** where it appeared that Lord Templeman unequivocally held that whether or not the claimant was an employee was a pure question of law.

The case of **Davies**, in which **O'Kelly** was not referred to, turned entirely upon the construction of a document, whereas **O'Kelly** had to be decided partly on the interpretation of various written documents and partly on inferences to be drawn from the parties' conduct. This difference was seized upon by the Court of Appeal in **Hellyer Brothers Ltd v McLeod** in order to distinguish **Davies** and to continue to apply the **O'Kelly** approach, viz an appellate court is entitled to interfere with the decision of an industrial tribunal on whether the applicant was employed under a contract of employment only if the tribunal had misdirected itself in law or its decision was one which no tribunal properly instructed could have reached.

More recently, the Privy Council in **Lee v Chung** adopted a similar approach to that taken in **McLeod**, holding that, in the ordinary case, whether or not a person is employed under a contract of employment is not a question of law but a question of fact to be determined by the industrial tribunal. **Davies v Presbyterian Church of Wales** was described as an exceptional case where the relationship was dependent solely on the construction of a written document.

Self-description of the employment relationship

After a period of uncertainty, where it was not clear whether the courts would allow the stated intentions of the parties to determine the matter of status, it now appears that the subjective intention of the parties will not override what in other respects has the attributes of a contract of employment.

In **Young & Woods Ltd v West**, West, a sheet worker, requested that he be treated as self-employed. This was accepted by his employer and, although there was no difference between his working conditions and those of the 'employees' he worked alongside, who did the same job under the same level of supervision, he was paid gross of tax. When West's job was terminated, he claimed that he was an employee after all and therefore entitled to claim unfair dismissal. The Court of Appeal held that, despite the arrangement with the employer, West was really an employee and the industrial tribunal had jurisdiction to hear his complaint.

Excluded categories of employment

Specific exclusions

Certain categories of employees are excluded by EPCA from the right to claim unfair dismissal. The most significant excluded groups are as follows:

- people employed in the police service (EPCA s145)
- members of the armed forces (EPCA s138)
- those covered by a dismissal procedure which is exempted from the legislation by ministerial order (EPCA s65)
- people on fixed-term contracts for at least one year who have waived their rights in writing (EPCA s142(1))
- those who ordinarily work outside the UK (EPCA s141)
- people excluded for reasons of national security (EPCA sch 9 para 2(1)).

Employees over retirement age

The EPCA s64(1)(b), as amended by the Sex Discrimination Act 1986, states that where there is a normal retirement age for employees holding the position in question which is the same for both men and women, then employees who have reached that age at the date of their dismissal will have no right to complain to a tribunal of unfair dismissal. If there is no such normal retirement age, then only employees aged 65 or over will be excluded.

There has been a trilogy of House of Lords' decisions on what constitutes 'normal retirement age'. It has been held that where the contract specifies a retirement age then this can be presumed to be the 'normal retiring age' (see *Nothman* v *Barnet LBC*). However, this presumption can be rebutted by evidence that the contractual age has been abandoned in practice. The test of whether this has happened is to 'ascertain what would be the reasonable expectation or understanding of employees holding that position at the relevant time' (*Waite* v *Government Communications Headquarters*).

The third decision made by the House of Lords, in *DHSS* v *Hughes*, concerned the question of whether employers can effectively alter a normal retirement age established by practice by a simple announcement to that effect. The House of Lords held that this was possible, since such an announcement would vary the expectations of those employees affected.

Insufficient continuity of employment

Employees who do not possess the requisite continuity of employment cannot bring a claim for unfair dismissal. Only in exceptional cases is no period of qualification required, as follows:

- dismissals related to union membership/activities
- refusal to join a union
- sex discrimination
- race discrimination.

In the vast majority of claims, therefore, the employee must be continuously employed for a period of two calendar years ending with the 'effective date of termination'.

The highly complex continuity rules are of fundamental relevance to claims for unfair dismissal and to the whole spectrum of employment protection rights. For this reason, they are discussed in some detail here.

The provisions relating to the calculation of a period of continuous employment are set out in EPCA sch 13. The schedule attempts to ensure that 'continuity' is preserved despite certain changes of employer, certain periods where the employee is away from work or where the employee's hours of work fluctuate.

Continuity: change of employer

In normal circumstances, only employment with the present employer counts towards continuity of employment. However, there are a number of circumstances set out in sch 13 paras 17 and 18 in which a change of employer does not break continuity. These include:

- a transfer which occurs on the death of an employer
- a change in the constitution of a partnership which acts as an employer
- where an Act of Parliament causes one corporate body to replace another as an employer.

However, the two most important situations provided for by sch 13 are:

1   If a trade, business or undertaking is transferred, the period of employment at the time of transfer counts as a period of employment with the transferee. In other words, the transfer does not break continuity (para 17(2)).

In order for this provision to operate the business must be transferred as a going concern; a mere sale of the physical assets of the business is insufficient. An example of this distinction is provided by *Woodhouse v Peter Brotherhood Ltd*. In this case, the nature of the business changed after the transfer from the manufacture of diesel engines to the manufacture of compressors and steam turbines. The Court of Appeal held that in this situation there was only a transfer of physical assets and not a transfer of a business.

In the important case of *Melon v Hector Powe Ltd*, Lord Frazer thought that the essential distinction between the transfer of a business or part of a business and the mere sale of assets was:

'that in the former case the business is transferred as a going concern so that the business remains the same business in different hands ... whereas in the latter case the assets are transferred to the new owner to be used in whatever business he chooses. Individual employees may continue to do the same work in the same environment and they may not appreciate that they are working in a different business, but that may be the true position on consideration of the whole circumstances.'

What counts as the essence of the business? In many cases a decisive factor will be the transfer of the 'goodwill', ie the acquisition of the right to trade with the transferor's former customers. Machinery, or other property, does not possess this essential quality. It is also likely that if the product changes after transfer then the 'business' has not been transferred.

In *Crompton v Truly Fair (International) Ltd*, for example, it was held that there was only a change of ownership of the physical assets. In this case, a factory, together with its machinery, was sold and was used for the manufacture of men's trousers, whereas the premises had originally been used for the manufacture of children's clothes.

Until recently, this provision was thought only to preserve continuity where the employee is employed in the business 'at the time of the transfer'. Consequently, a gap between the employee's employment with the transferor and employment with the transferee would break continuity. In **Macer v Abafast**, the EAT adopted an alternative purposive interpretation of this provision, and held that periods of employment accrued with the old employer at the time of the transfer could be added to the period of employment with the new employer, and that any gap in employment 'which is related to the machinery of transfer' should not break continuity.

In **Macer**, it was admitted that the new owners had deliberately attempted to break the applicant's continuity by creating a gap of more than one week before the transfer transactions commenced. The EAT decided that continuity was preserved and that the applicant was entitled to maintain his claim for unfair dismissal.

In approaching the construction of the provison, the EAT felt that:

'the Court should lean in favour of that interpretation which best gives effect to the preservation of continuity of service and hence to the rights of the employee, and to obviate and discourage a tactical manoeuvre which seeks to avoid the clear intention of Parliament.'

2   If the employee is taken into the employment of an 'associated employer', the period of employment with the old employer counts as a period of employment with the 'associated employer' (para 18).

The definition of this concept is to be found in EPCA s153(4) which states that '. . . any two employers are to be treated as associated if one is a company of which the other (directly or indirectly) has control, or if both are companies of which a third person (directly or indirectly) has control'.

Two major issues arise from this definition. First, 'control' means voting control rather than *de facto* control. In **Secretary of State for Employment v Newbold**, Mr Justice Bristow stated:

'In the law affecting companies, control is well recognised to mean control by the majority of votes attaching to the shares exercised in General Meeting. It is not how or by whom the enterprise is actually run.'

Second, the definition has been held to be exhaustive, so that only companies can be associated – local authorities or health authorities fall outside the definition (see *Gardiner* v *London Borough of Merton*).

In *Hancill* v *Marcon Engineering Ltd*, it was held that the word 'company' in s153(4) can include an overseas company if the overseas company can be likened in its essentials to a company limited under the Companies Acts. Thus, Mr Hancill was able to count his period of employment with an American subsidiary in order to meet the qualifying period of service for claiming unfair dismissal.

The Transfer of Undertakings (Protection of Employment) Regulations 1981

These complex regulations (SI 1981 No 1794) implement additional rules to protect the employee's rights where there is a change of employer. They provide for the automatic transfer of contracts of employment, collective agreements and trade union recognition in the case of certain transfers of commercial ventures, impose a duty on employers to inform and consult recognised trade unions and hold any dismissal in connection with such transfers automatically unfair unless it occurs for an 'economic, technical or organisational' reason. This latter aspect of the regulations will be discussed in greater detail in chapter 6.

A relevant transfer

None of the provisions of the 1981 Regulations operate unless there is a 'relevant transfer' under reg 3(1), ie 'a transfer from one person to another of an undertaking situated immediately before the transfer in the UK or a part of one so situated'. An undertaking is defined by reg 2(1) to include 'any trade or business but does not include any undertaking or part of an undertaking which is not in the nature of a commercial venture'. It would appear that, as under EPCA sch 13 para 17(2), a mere transfer of assets which falls short of a transfer of the business as a going concern, will fall outside the regulations.

The effect of a transfer on the contract of employment

The important change provided for in the regulations is that the common law position is overridden so that a transfer does not terminate the contracts of the employees of the business. Instead, contracts continue with the substitution of the transferee as employer and the transferee taking all the transferor's 'rights, powers, duties and liabilities under or in connection with any such contract' (reg 5(1) and (2)).

By virtue of reg 5(3), however, this transfer of liability will only occur where the employee was employed in the undertaking 'immediately before the transfer'.

Different divisions of the EAT reached different conclusions on the precise interpretation of the phrase 'immediately before the transfer'. This conflict of authority was apparently resolved by the decision of the Court of Appeal in *Secretary of State for Employment* v *Spence* that only when employees are employed at the very moment of a business transfer does the purchaser take over the vendor's liabilities under or in connection with their employment contracts. In other words, a business purchaser could not be made liable for dismissals carried out by the vendor before the transfer.

The scope of this decision is now heavily constrained by the very recent judgement of the House of Lords in *Litster* v *Forth Dry Dock & Engineering Co Ltd*. The House of Lords held that liability for a dismissal by the vendor prior to the transfer passes to the purchaser if the employee has been unfairly dismissed for a reason connected with the transfer.

Although reg 5(3) provides that liability is to be transferred only where the employee is 'employed immediately before the transfer', in order for the regulations to give effect to the EC Council Employee Rights On Transfer Of Business Directive 77/187 as interpreted by the European Court of Justice, reg 5(3) must be read as if there were inserted the words 'or would have been so employed if he had not been unfairly dismissed in the circumstances described in reg 8(1)'.

Without such a purposive interpretation, the regulations would, according to Lord Keith, 'be capable of ready evasion through the transferee arranging with the transferor for the latter to dismiss its employees a short time before the transfer becomes operative', thereby leaving the employees, as in this case, with 'worthless claims for unfair dismissal' against an insolvent vendor (see *P Bork International A/S v Forgeningen af Arbejdsledere i Danmark*).

The approach advocated by the House of Lords is two-fold:

1 It must be determined whether the dismissal by the vendor was unfair within the meaning of reg 8. If yes, then unfair dismissal liability under reg 5 passes to the purchaser, even if the dismissal was not, in temporal terms, immediately before the transfer.

2 It is only where the dismissal does not breach reg 8 that the construction of 'employed immediately before the transfer' laid down in *Spence* continues to apply. So, if the reason for the dismissal is unconnected with the transfer, liability passes to the transferee only if the employee had been dismissed after the moment of transfer.

Continuity: periods away from work

An employee's service may be continuous in a statutory sense even where the employee has been away from work for certain periods.

The EPCA sch 13 para 4, makes it clear that each week during which there is in existence a contract of employment that would normally involve employment for 16 hours or more per week, counts as a week of continuous employment. This is so whether the employee is actually at work or not. It follows that periods of absence from work by reason of sickness or pregnancy will count as periods of continuous employment without reliance on any other provision so long as the contract of employment has not been terminated.

Even where an employee is away from work and no longer has a contract, service may still be deemed to be continuous in certain situations should the employee eventually return to work. These situations are set out in sch 13, paras 9 and 10:

1 Absence through sickness or injury, provided the absence does not exceed 26 weeks.

2   Up to 26 weeks' absence wholly or partly because of pregnancy or confinement (eg where a woman with less than two years' service with her employer has been dismissed fairly while absent because of pregnancy and is later re-employed by that employer.

3   The whole of statutory permitted absence for leave on the grounds of pregnancy or confinement.

4   Absence through a 'temporary cessation of work'.

This phrase has caused some difficulty – two decisions by the House of Lords and one by the Court of Appeal have provided guidance on its interpretation. The first authority is *Fitzgerald* v *Hall Russell Ltd,* where it was held that the phrase refers to the cessation of the individual employee's work for some reason – there is no need to show that 'at the same time the whole works would close down or a department was closed down or a large number of other employees were laid off at the same time' (Lord Upjohn).

This decision also states that in order to determine whether the absence is temporary it should be viewed in the context of the employment relationship as a whole. With the benefit of hindsight, it should be possible to establish whether the absence was of a transient nature.

In the later decision of *Ford* v *Warwickshire County Council,* the applicant was a teacher who had been employed by the County Council under a series of consecutive short-term contracts, each for an academic year, for a total of eight years. There was, therefore, a break between the end of one contract and the beginning of the next. The House of Lords held that para 9(1)(b) could apply in order to preserve the continuity of her employment. In the course of his judgement, Lord Diplock offered the following guidance:

'The continuity of employment for the purpose of the Act is not broken unless and until looking backwards from the date of the expiry of the fixed-term contract on which the employee's claim is based, there is to be found between one fixed-term contract and its immediate predecessor an interval that cannot be characterised as short relative to the combined duration of the two fixed-term contracts.'

This approach is undoubtedly of benefit to many employees, such as part-time or temporary teachers, and makes it much more difficult for employers to avoid the employment protection laws by offering a succession of fixed-term contracts. However, it may not be appropriate where patterns of employment are not regular, as they were in Ford's case, but are subject to fluctuation. To look only at a particular period of unemployment and to compare that period with the combination of the periods either side could lead to some unjust results.

This issue arose before the Court of Appeal in *Flack v Kodak Ltd*. In this case, Mrs Flack had been employed by Kodak in their photo-finishing department over a number of years for periods which fluctuated markedly. Following her final dismissal, she and the other 'seasonal employees' claimed redundancy payments.

An industrial tribunal, purporting to follow what Lord Diplock had said in *Ford* with regard to temporary cessation, rejected their claim. In coming to this conclusion, the tribunal confined itself to a purely mathematical comparison of each gap in employment falling within the two years preceding the final dismissal, with the period of employment immediately before and after that gap.

Both the EAT and Court of Appeal thought that this was the wrong approach in the context of this particular case. They were of the view that the correct approach was to take into account all the relevant circumstances, and in particular consider the length of the period of employment as a whole. It was true that the only absences from work on account of temporary cessations of work which were relevant for the purposes of redundancy payments and unfair dismissal claim qualifications, were those which occurred during the two years prior to the dismissal. However, the characterisations of those cessations as temporary may be crucially affected by the whole history of the employment. As Sir John Donaldson put it:

'A long gap in the course of a longer period of work extending over many years might well be considered temporary, whereas if the same gap occurred in the course of a shorter period it would not.'

5   Absence from work 'in circumstances such that, by arrangement or custom', the employee is regarded as continuing in the employment of the employer for all or any purposes.

It would appear that in order to fall within this provision, the arrangement or understanding must be established at the time the absence commences and cannot be agreed retrospectively (see, for example, *Murphy* v *A Birrell & Sons*). The absences that might be encompassed could be leave of absence arrangements, employees placed upon a 'reserve list' to be called upon as necessary and employees on secondment.

A number of commentators argue that the EAT's broad application of the sub-paragraph in *Lloyds Bank Ltd* v *Secretary of State for Employment* is no longer good law following the judgement of the Lords in *Ford*. In the *Lloyds* case, the EAT held that where an employee works on a one week on and one week off basis, the weeks which she does not work count towards continuity by virtue of para 9(1)(c). This was despite the fact that the side note to para 9 reads 'Periods in which there is no contract of employment'. In the *Lloyds* case a contract did exist throughout the period of employment. In the *Ford* case, the House of Lords placed considerable emphasis on the requirement that there be no subsisting contract before para 9 could operate. On that basis, the authority of the *Lloyds* case looks decidedly shaky.

Strikes and lockouts

If an employee takes part in a strike or a lockout, the beginning of the period of employment is treated as postponed by the number of days between the start of the strike or lockout and the resumption of work (para 15). In other words, the period of the industrial dispute does not count towards continuity, but it does not break it.

Continuity: changes in hours of work

For a week of employment to count for the purpose of calculating continuous service, the employee must either actually work (para 3), or be employed under a contract of employment normally involving 16 hours per week (para 4). Employees who cannot meet this criterion will only cross this particular threshold of employment law rights after five years' continuous employment at eight hours or more per week (para 6).

Employees whose weekly hours fluctuate above and below the hours threshold are not allowed to 'average' (see *Opie* v *John*

Gubbins (Insurance Brokers) Ltd) and, in general, if weekly hours fall below the relevant eight or 16 hours per week, continuity will be broken and the employee will be back at 'square one' in attempting to qualify for employment protection (see paras 5 and 7 for the two exceptions to this rule).

An important recent decision in this area is that of the House of Lords in *Lewis* v *Surrey County Council*, where the House of Lords held that where an employee is employed under separate but concurrent part-time contracts, she is not entitled to aggregate the number of weekly hours worked under each contract for continuity purposes.

Presentation of claim in time

In common with the enforcement of other employment protection rights, an applicant must present a claim (using an IT1 form) to the Central Office of Industrial Tribunals within three months of the effective date of termination. This time limit is fairly rigorously applied, although EPCA s67(2) confers upon tribunals a discretion to allow a claim to be presented within a reasonable time outside the three month period where it considers that it was not reasonably practicable for the complaint to be presented in time.

The leading authorities in this area state that the test to be applied in determining whether a late claim should be considered is not confined to whether the applicant knew of the right to claim, but extends to a consideration as to whether he or she should have known (*Dedman* v *British Building & Engineering Appliances*; *Walls Meat Co Ltd* v *Khan*). In other words, ignorance of rights is not an excuse, unless it appears that the applicant could not reasonably be expected to be aware of them. Such is the stringency of the rule that it has been held that an applicant may not use the excuse that his or her failure to claim in time was due to a mistake of a 'skilled adviser' such as a lawyer, trade union official or Citizens' Advice Bureau employee (*Riley* v *Tesco Stores Ltd*).

However, in *Jean Sorelle Ltd* v *Rybak*, the EAT held that there is a clear factual difference between, on the one hand, advice obtained from someone who is asked, whether for a fee or not, to advise the applicant in the presentation of a claim against the employer and, on the other hand, advice obtained from an industrial tribunal employee. Therefore, the fact that Ms Rybak was given erroneous advice concerning the final date for presentation of her claim by an industrial tribunal clerk provided grounds to excuse her late claim.

One recurring problem in this area is the question as to whether it is reasonable for the applicant to delay making a claim until the outcome of an internal appeal is known. The balance of authority would now suggest that this would not be a reason for admitting a late claim (see *Palmer* v *Southend-on-Sea Borough Council*).

Examples of valid reasons for delay might be physical incapacity, absence abroad or a postal strike (given as examples in *Walls Meat Co Ltd* v *Khan* (above)). If an employee does not discover a fundamental fact until more than three months after the date of dismissal an extension may also be granted. This was the approach taken by the EAT in *Churchill* v *Yeates & Son Ltd*, where the applicant did not discover evidence that his dismissal purportedly for redundancy may have been a sham until after the three month deadline.

The decision in *Churchill* has more recently received the approval of the House of Lords in *Machine Tool Industry Research Association* v *Simpson*. It is difficult to offer much more guidance on this point because the Court of Appeal has made it clear that the application of the exemption is essentially a matter of fact for the tribunal to decide whether it was 'reasonably feasible' to claim in time (see *Palmer* v *Southend-on-Sea Borough Council* (above)).

The effective date of termination (EDT)

It is essential to identify the date of termination. This will determine:

- whether a claim is made in time
- whether the applicant possessed the requisite continuity of employment at the date of dismissal
- whether the retirement age exclusion is to operate in any particular case
- from when to calculate compensation if the claim is successful.

The EPCA provides a definition of the date of termination for both unfair dismissal and redundancy payment claims and, although for unfair dismissal purposes it is called the 'effective date of termination' and for redundancy payments 'the relevant date', the definition is largely the same in both cases (see EPCA ss55(4) and 90(1)).

1   Where the contract of employment is terminated by notice, whether by employer or employee, the date of termination is the date on which the notice expires.

Where notice is given orally on a day when work is carried out, the notice period does not begin to run until the following day (**West** v **Kneels Ltd**). If an employee is dismissed *with notice* but is given a payment in lieu of working out that notice, the EDT is the date when the notice expires (**Adams** v **GKN Sankey**). As will be seen below, a fine distinction is drawn between the latter situation and one where the employee is dismissed *with no notice*, with the payment being made in lieu of notice.

2   Where the contract of employment is terminated without notice, the date of termination is the date on which the termination takes effect.

Two useful cases in this area are **Robert Cort & Sons** v **Charman** and **Stapp** v **The Shaftesbury Society**, which both uphold the view that the effective date of termination is the actual date of termination regardless of whether the employment was lawfully or unlawfully terminated. So where, as in **Cort**, an employee is immediately dismissed with wages in lieu of notice, the effective date of termination is the actual date on which the employee is told of dismissal and not the date on which notice would expire.

The only exception to this rule is provided by s55(5) which artificially extends the EDT, either where summary dismissal has occurred despite a period of statutory minimum notice being due under s49, or where the statutory notice required to be given is longer than the actual notice given. In either case, the date of the ending of the s49 notice period is treated as the EDT.

An unresolved problem is whether the s55(5) extension of the EDT will apply in the event of a dismissal for 'gross misconduct'. This doubt arises because s49(5) declares that the minimum notice entitlement under the section 'does not affect any right of either party to treat the contract as terminable without notice by reason of such conduct by the other party as would have enabled him to so treat it before the passing of this Act'.

The only authority on this point is **Lanton Leisure Ltd** v **White and Gibson**. In this case, the EAT ruled that an employer cannot avoid the effect of s55(5) merely by dismissing summarily and labelling the reason for dismissal as gross misconduct. The EAT decided that, in such a case, 'it is first necessary to find out by means of an enquiry on the merits whether there was in fact such conduct which would enable an employer to terminate without notice'. Since the tribunal's decision on whether there has been conduct meriting summary dismissal will be virtually the same as whether the dismissal was fair or unfair, it would appear that in practice s49(5) does not prevent the operation of s55(5).

3   Where the employee is employed under a contract for a fixed-term, the date of termination is the date on which the term expires.

Internal appeals and the effective date of termination

Where the dismissed employee exercises a right of appeal in accordance with the company's internal or disciplinary appeals procedure, the question may arise as to whether the EDT becomes the date of the determination of the appeal, or whether the original date of dismissal still stands as the EDT.

The leading authority on this question is the Court of Appeal's decision in **J Sainsbury Ltd** v **Savage**, where it was held that if the dismissed employee invokes an internal appeal which is subsequently rejected, the EDT is the date of the original dismissal, unless the contract provides to the contrary. This approach was expressly approved by the House of Lords in the important case of **West Midlands Co-operative Society** v **Tipton** which is discussed in more detail in chapter 5.

4 THE EMPLOYER'S REASON FOR DISMISSAL

It is for the employer to establish that there was an 'admissible' reason for dismissal (EPCA s57(1) and (2)). These may be as follows:

- capability or qualifications
- conduct
- redundancy
- that the employee could not continue to work without contravention of a statute
- some other substantial reason.

The reasons for dismissal will always raise complex issues in the event of a claim of unfair dismissal and these categories of admissible reasons are dealt with in detail in chapter 6. Initially, however, justifying the dismissal by providing a reason, or principal reason for it will not be difficult since at this stage there is no consideration of fairness. The fact that an employer wrongly labels a capability dismissal as one for redundancy probably will not tell against the employer's case given that the legal definition is considerably more restricted than the layperson's understanding of it. What then must be proved is the employer's subjective motivation for dismissal. As Lord Justice Cairns put it in *Abernethy* v *Mott Hay and Anderson*:

'A reason for the dismissal of an employee is a set of facts known to the employer or beliefs held by him which cause him to dismiss the employee.'

If an employer gives several reasons for dismissal and one of the reasons is not made out, the burden is on the employer to show that the reason formed 'no important part' of the reason or principal reason for the dismissal (see *Smith* v *City of Glasgow District Council*).

An employer will only be allowed to rely upon facts known at the time of dismissal to establish what was the reason for the dismissal.

Facts which come to light after the dismissal cannot be relied to justify the dismissal. This was the conclusion of the House of Lords in the important case of *W Devis & Sons Ltd* v *Atkins*.

The employee was dismissed because of his refusal to comply with his employer's wishes. The employer subsequently discovered that the employee had been guilty of serious misconduct. At the hearing of the employee's unfair dismissal claim the employers sought to adduce evidence of his misconduct to show that they had acted reasonably in the circumstances in dismissing the employee. Permission was refused. The House of Lords upheld the tribunal's decision and held that it was not possible, without doing great damage to its language, to construe the wording of what is now s57(3) as enabling the tribunal to have regard to matters which the employer was unaware of at the time of the dismissal, and which therefore could not have formed part of the reason or reasons for dismissing the employee.

The written statement of reasons for dismissal

In order to maintain credibility, the employer should maintain a consistent story throughout the proceedings. In this regard it is important to note that EPCA s53 provides that an employee who is under notice or who has been dismissed has a right to be provided by the employer with a written statement of reasons for the dismissal. Once a dismissed employee asks for written reasons, the employer is required to supply them within 14 days of the request.

The Employment Act 1989 s15 has increased the period of continuous employment necessary for ex-employees to exercise this right from six months to two years. The procedural significance of s53 is that a written statement provided under the section is expressly made admissible in subsequent proceedings. Any basic inconsistency between the terms of the statement and the reason actually put forward before the tribunal could seriously undermine the employer's case.

If an employer unreasonably refuses to comply with the request or provides particulars which are 'inadequate or untrue', the employee may present a complaint to an industrial tribunal, which may declare what it finds the reasons for dismissal are and also make an award of two weeks' wages to the employee.

The statement provided by the employer must contain at least a simple statement of the essential reasons for the dismissal, but no particular form is required. Indeed, it has been held that it is acceptable for a written statement to refer the employee to earlier correspondence which contains the reasons for dismissal and attaching a copy of that correspondence (**Kent County Council v Gilham & Others**).

It does not matter whether the reason put forward by the employer is 'intrinsically a good, bad or indifferent one'; at this stage the industrial tribunal is concerned only with identifying a genuine reason for the dismissal. So, in **Harvard Securities plc v Younghusband**, where the employers stated that they had dismissed the employee for divulging confidential information to a third party, whether the employers were correct in describing that information as 'confidential' was irrelevant to the identification of their reason for dismissal.

Pressure on an employer to dismiss

The EPCA s63 states that, in determining the reason for the dismissal and its fairness, no account shall be taken of any industrial pressure (official or unofficial) exerted on the employer to dismiss the employee. It follows that if an employer cannot advance any reason other than the industrial pressure the dismissal will be held to be unfair.

Nevertheless, a trade union or union official who has exerted pressure to force the employer to dismiss a non-union member, may be joined in subsequent unfair dismissal proceedings and be ordered to pay all or part of any compensation awarded (EPCA s76A).

Reasons for dismissal which are deemed to be unfair

Certain reasons for dismissal are regarded as automatically unfair. These are as follows:

1 Dismissal for trade union membership and activity, or because of refusal to join a trade union or particular trade union (EPCA s58 as amended by the Employment Act 1988 s11).

The following two cases provide contrasting examples of judicial approaches to trade union membership discrimination. In **Therm A Stor Ltd v Atkins**, a large majority of the shopfloor workforce applied to join the union. The company's response to the union's claim for recognition was to dismiss 20 employees. The selection was left to chargehands and, although there was no evidence that the selections were made on the basis of union membership, all those selected for dismissal were union members. The Court of Appeal held that the dismissals fell outside the section because they were in response to the union's claim for recognition and *not* because of any of the dismissed individuals' union membership or activities.

In ***Discount Tobacco & Confectionery Ltd* v *Armitage***, we see a more liberal approach to the scope of s58. Mrs Armitage enlisted the help of her union official in order to clarify her terms and conditions of employment. The employers then dismissed her. Mrs Armitage claimed that she had been dismissed because of her trade union membership so that, notwithstanding that she had worked for the company for only a very short time (around five and a half months), she was entitled to a finding that her dismissal was unfair (s58(1)(a)). The employers argued that there was a distinction between union membership on the one hand and seeking the assistance of the union official on the other, and that dismissal for the latter reason was not caught by the section.

This view was rejected by the EAT. It was stated that:

> 'the activities of a trade union officer in negotiating and elucidating terms of employment is . . . the outward and visible manifestation of trade union membership. It is an incident of union membership which is, if not the primary one, at any rate, a very important one and we see no genuine distinction between membership of a union on the one hand and making use of the essential services of a union on the other . . . Were it not so, the scope of s58(1)(a) would be reduced almost to vanishing point . . . .'

Most cases arising under this section involve the question of whether the dismissal was for taking part in the activities of a trade union at an appropriate time (EPCA s58(1)(b)). The scope of the trade union activities protected by the sub-section has been viewed restrictively by the courts. It has been held that the personal activities of a union member are not the activities of a trade union within the meaning of s58. For example, in ***Chant* v *Aquaboats Ltd***, a union member who organised a petition complaining about safety standards was held not to be engaged in trade union activity, notwithstanding the fact that a union official had vetted the petition before it was presented. The EAT stated:

'The mere fact that one or two of the employees making representations happen to be trade unionists, and the mere fact that the spokesman of the men happens to be a trade unionist does not make such representations a trade union activity.'

The courts and tribunals have tended to require that the activity is connected with the institutional aspects of trade unions, such as taking part in trade union meetings, distributing union material, recruiting a fellow employee or consulting a trade union official.

For trade union activity to be protected it must take place at 'an appropriate time'. This is defined as not only occasions 'outside the employee's working hours' but also time 'within working hours at which, in accordance with arrangements agreed with or consent given by his employer, it is permissible for him to take part in those activities' (EPCA s58(2)). Working hours means hours when, in accordance with an employee's contract, he or she is required to be at work. It has been held that 'periods when in accordance with his contract the worker is on his employer's premises but not actually working' are outside 'working hours' (Lord Reid in *The Post Office* v *UPW*). Consequently, the view has been taken that a paid meal break is not a time within working hours which requires the employer's consent to take part in trade union activities (*Zucker* v *Astrid Jewels*).

Where the activities take place within working hours, it must be by the consent of the employer. Consent may be expressed or implied. In *Zucker*, for example, the employee alleged that he had been dismissed for discussing trade union matters while working on a machine, and encouraging union recruitment during meal breaks. The EAT held that such conduct could constitute trade union activities at an appropriate time, for the employees were permitted to converse during working hours, and consequently they had an implied right to discuss trade union matters. However, in *Marley Tile Co Ltd* v *Shaw*, the Court of Appeal was not prepared to imply the employer's consent from his silence in response to the announcement of an unaccredited shop steward that he would be calling a meeting during working hours.

In **Drew v St Edmundsbury Borough Council** it was held that taking part in industrial action does not constitute taking part in the activities of an independent trade union within the meaning of s58 and, as we shall see below, a dismissal for that reason may not be challenged at all if it comes within EPCA s62.

Finally, in **Birmingham City District Council v Beyer**, the EAT took the view that s58 only applies to trade union activities which take place after employment with a particular employer has commenced and 'could not conceivably refer to activities before the employment began'. The Employment Act 1990 s1(1) now makes it unlawful to refuse a person employment because he or she is, or is not, a member of a trade union. However, it may be argued that the provision will still not prevent an employer from excluding a candidate on the grounds of past 'activities' or because he or she is regarded as a 'troublemaker'.

2   Dismissal of a woman because she is pregnant or for a reason connected with her pregnancy (EPCA s60).

However, it will not be automatically unfair to dismiss in such circumstances if the dismissal was for one of the following two reasons:

- that at the effective date of termination she is or will have become, because of her pregnancy, incapable of doing the work which she is employed to do or
- that, because of her pregnancy, she cannot or will not be able to continue after that date to do that work without contravention (either by her or by her employer) of a duty or restriction imposed by or under any enactment.

If the employer is to be able to rely on one or other of these exceptions, he or she must show that the pregnant employee was offered suitable alternative employment or that no suitable alternative employment was available.

See **Brown v Stockton-on-Tees Borough Council**, where the House of Lords decided that selection for redundancy on grounds of pregnancy is dismissal for a 'reason connected with her pregnancy' within the meaning of EPCA s60.

'If an employer dismisses a woman because she is pregnant and is not prepared to make the arrangements to cover her temporary absence from work he is deemed to have dismissed her unfairly. I can see no reason why the same principle should not apply if in a redundancy situation an employer selects the pregnant woman as the victim of redundancy in order to avoid the inconvenience of covering her absence from work in the new employment he is able to offer to others who are threatened with redundancy. It surely cannot have been intended that an employer should be entitled to take advantage of a redundancy situation to weed out his pregnant employees.' (Lord Griffiths)

So even if redundancy is the reason for the dismissal, it is still 'connected with pregnancy' if pregnancy is the reason for the selection for redundancy.

The reasoning in **Brown** was applied by the EAT in **Clayton v Vigers**. Mrs Vigers was employed as a dental assistant to Mr Clayton. She was dismissed by her employer during her maternity leave because he was unable to make temporary arrangements to cover her absence from work. In upholding the industrial tribunal's finding of unfair dismissal, the EAT stated that the words 'any other reason connected with her pregnancy' in s60 should be 'read widely so as to give full effect to the mischief at which the statute was aimed'. Therefore, it is sufficient if the reason for or the dismissal is 'associated with pregnancy' or the after-effects of pregnancy.

Protection under EPCA s60 is available only to women with two years' continuous service. However, if a woman does not have the necessary qualifying service, she can still challenge a pregnancy dismissal by way of the sex discrimination legislation. According to UK case law so far, she must then show that a man in comparable circumstances (eg one who was going to be absent for health reasons) would have been treated better than she was (**Webb v EMO Air Cargo Ltd**).

However, the decision of the European Court of Justice in **Dekker v Stichting Vormingscentrum voor Jong Volvassen (VJW-Centrum) Plus** offers greater protection to pregnant women. In this case, the European Court of Justice held that unfavourable treatment on grounds of pregnancy was direct discrimination on grounds of sex. The Court reasoned that pregnancy is a condition unique to women, so that where it can be shown that unfavourable treatment is on the grounds of pregnancy, that treatment is, by definition, on grounds of sex. A reason which applies 'exclusively to one sex' – in effect a sex-based classification – is in effect inherently discriminatory. Since discrimination on grounds of pregnancy is discrimination on grounds of sex *per se*, there is no need to compare the treatment of a pregnant woman with that of a hypothetical man.

The import of this decision is as follows. An employer who refuses to hire or promote, or dismisses a woman who is otherwise suitable because she is pregnant or for a reason based on her pregnancy, is directly discriminating. It should follow that, to the extent that supremacy must be accorded to the European Court's decision, the comparative approach to pregnancy discrimination that like must be compared with like, which was followed by the EAT in *Webb*, is no longer good law. It should not, therefore, be followed by the industrial tribunals. This is because it is a fundamental principle of EC law that national courts are bound to interpret national law in the light of the aim of an EC Directive as interpreted by the ECJ.

3   Dismissal because of a conviction which is 'spent' under the terms of the Rehabilitation of Offenders Act 1974 (see s4(3)(b) and the discussion in chapter 6).

4   Dismissal connected with the transfer of an undertaking unless there are 'economic, technical or organisational' reasons entailing changes in the workforce (see the Transfer of Undertakings Regulations 1981 reg 8 and the discussion in chapter 6).

5   Unfair redundancy selection (see EPCA s59).

The dismissal of an employee on the grounds of redundancy will be unfair if the circumstances constituting the redundancy applied equally to one or more employees in the same undertaking who held posts similar to that held by the dismissed employee and who had not been dismissed by the employer, and either:

• the reason (or, if more than one, the principal reason) for which he or she was selected was union-related *or*

- the employee was selected for dismissal in contravention of a customary arrangement or agreed procedure relating to redundancy, and there were no special reasons justifying a departure from that arrangement or procedure in the circumstances of the case.

No right to claim for those taking industrial action

Where dismissal is for taking part in a strike or other industrial action, where all those still on strike have been dismissed and there has been no selective re-engagement of those dismissed within a three month period, statute prevents an industrial tribunal from hearing an unfair dismissal claim (EPCA s62).

'Other industrial action' is not defined by the Act but it is now clear that it can encompass forms of action which do not constitute a breach of the contract of employment. In *Faust v Power Packing Casemakers Ltd*, in which three employees refused to work overtime because of a dispute over wages, the industrial tribunal had found the dismissals unfair on the grounds that there was no contractual obligation to work overtime. Both the EAT and the Court of Appeal rejected this view stating that any action taken against an employer during the course of a dispute which was designed to extract some benefit from him or her constituted 'other industrial action' – whether or not it was in breach of contract.

In determining whether there has been a selective dismissal or re-engagement of strikers, the tribunal must have regard to the 'relevant employees'. These are defined as those employees at the establishment who were taking part in the industrial action at the date of the applicant's dismissal. In other words, those who have been on strike but who have returned to work before that date are not included and the fact that they are not dismissed does not entitle the dismissed employees to present a claim.

The time at which it must be shown that one or more 'relevant employees' who took part in a strike were not dismissed, for the purposes of deciding whether an industrial tribunal has jurisdiction to hear the unfair dismissal claim, is the conclusion of the relevant hearing at which the tribunal determines whether it has jurisdiction (*P&O European Ferries (Dover) Ltd v Byrne*). This is an extremely favourable interpretation for employers because if the identities of those strikers whom the employer has, by mistake, failed to dismiss are revealed during the proceedings, then the employer can escape liability by dismissing them before the conclusion of those proceedings.

Whether a particular employee is taking part in a strike within the meaning of s62 is a question of fact for the industrial tribunal to decide. In *Coates* v *Modern Methods and Materials Ltd*, however, the majority of the Court of Appeal expressed the view that the matter should be judged by what the employee does and not by what he or she thinks or why he or she does it. Reasons or motives are irrelevant. Therefore, an employee who does not support the strike but who does not cross the picket line because of fear of abuse could reasonably be regarded as taking part in the strike.

The Employment Act 1990 s9(1) adds a new section 62(A) to the EPCA. The effect of this amendment is that, henceforth, no employee can complain of unfair dismissal if at the time of the dismissal he or she was taking part in unofficial industrial action. In such a situation the employer may selectively dismiss or re-engage any participating employee without risking unfair dismissal liability.

An employee's action will be unofficial unless:

- he or she is a member of a trade union and the action is authorised and endorsed by that union *or*
- he or she is not a trade union member, but a member of a union which has authorised or endorsed the action also take part *or*
- no trade union members are taking part in the industrial action.

5 DID THE EMPLOYER ACT REASONABLY?

Prior to 1980, the burden of proof in unfair dismissal claims at this stage was on the employer. Section 6 of the Employment Act 1980 amended EPCA s57(3) primarily by removing the requirement that the employer *shall* satisfy the industrial tribunal as to the reasonableness of his or her action and so rendered the burden of proof 'neutral'. Section 6 also required tribunals to have regard to the size and administrative resources of the employer's undertaking in assessing the reasonableness of the dismissal.

In applying the test of reasonableness, the question is what a reasonable employer would have done in the circumstances and not what a particular tribunal would have thought right. As such, the reasonableness test is viewed by a number of commentators as not unduly challenging managerial prerogatives in the matter of discipline. In its current formulation, the test is whether the dismissal fell within 'the band of reasonable responses to the employee's conduct within which one employer might take one view, another quite reasonably another' (President Browne-Wilkinson in *Iceland Frozen Foods* v *Jones*).

Provided the industrial tribunal follows the 'band of reasonable responses' test and does not substitute its own view, it will have considerable discretion in reaching its decision and it will only be in rare cases that its decision will be overturned on appeal. This is because the fairness of the dismissal is essentially a question of fact and, so long as the industrial tribunal has properly directed itself as to the law, then its decision will only be overturned if it was perverse, ie that no reasonable tribunal could possibly have come to that decision on the particular facts.

In reaching a conclusion on the reasonableness of the dismissal, the tribunal may have regard to two broad questions – the substantive merits and procedural fairness.

The substantive merits

This involves the tribunal taking into account mitigating factors such as the employee's length of service, previous disciplinary record and any explanation or excuse. It is also important to maintain consistency in the application of disciplinary rules so that employees who behave in much the same way should have meted out to them much the same punishment. In *The Post Office v Fennell*, the employee was instantly dismissed following an assault on a fellow employee in the works canteen. The Court of Appeal upheld a finding of unfair dismissal on the grounds that there was evidence that other employees had been guilty of similar offences but these had not been met by dismissal.

The principle of consistency, however, should not be interpreted so as to force the employer merely to adopt a 'tariff' approach to misconduct and apply rules in an inflexible manner – the mitigating factors in each individual case should be fully considered before deciding whether the circumstances are truly parallel (*Hadjioannou v Coral Casinos Ltd*).

Inconsistency of treatment in relation to those fighting at work was again an issue in *Cain v Leeds Western Health Authority*. The applicant, who worked in a hospital laundry, was dismissed on the grounds of misconduct for fighting with another employee while on duty. Mr Cain claimed that his dismissal was unfair, because in the past other employees guilty of acts of gross misconduct, including fighting, had not been dismissed.

The industrial tribunal, in dismissing his complaint, disregarded the inconsistencies in treatment on the grounds that the relevant decisions in the various cases were taken by different members of management. This view was overturned by the EAT who held that it is inconsistency of treatment by the *employer* rather than by individual line managers that is the crucial question:

'Because an employer is acting in one case through his servants A and B, and the other case through his servants C and D, it is no answer to a complaint of unfair dismissal to say that there were different employees considering the seriousness of the two alleged cases of misconduct. The consistency must be consistency as between all the employees of the employer.'

Procedural fairness

The second element of the test of fairness relates to the question of the fairness of the procedures adopted by the employer in the events leading up to the dismissal. The concept of procedural fairness is not expressly articulated in the legislation, but its development was influenced by the codes of practice which were introduced to accompany the legislation. The provisions relevant to discipline and dismissal are presently contained in the ACAS Code of Practice No 1 *Disciplinary Practices & Procedures in Employment*. The Code's guidelines do not carry the force of law but any of its provisions which appear to a court or tribunal to be relevant to a question arising in the proceedings must be taken into account in reaching a decision (see Employment Protection Act 1975 s6(11)).

In 1987, ACAS produced an updated and enlarged draft code of practice for the consideration of Lord Young, the then Secretary of State for Employment. The draft code offered advice on the handling of dismissals in general, together with more detailed consideration of common types of disciplinary problems such as absenteeism, sub-standard work and dishonesty. This guidance was based on the principles which had emerged from 15 years of unfair dismissal case law. Unfortunately, the draft code was rejected by Lord Young because he thought it over-lengthy and too detailed, 'aimed primarily at lawyers and personnel managers in larger firms', and incapable of application by a small employer.

Following rejection of the draft code, ACAS published much of the material it contained in the form of an advisory handbook entitled *Discipline At Work*. Though this handbook has no statutory force, given that it concisely summarises the views of the leading cases on what constitutes good disciplinary practice, it is well worthy of careful study and may well be influential in industrial tribunal adjudications.

Essential features of disciplinary procedures

The ACAS Code of Practice emphasises that disciplinary procedures should not be viewed primarily as a means of imposing sanctions; they should also be designed to emphasise and encourage improvements in individual conduct.

Paragraph 10 of the Code recommends that disciplinary procedures should:

- Be in writing.
- Specify to whom they apply.
- Provide for matters to be dealt with quickly.
- Indicate the disciplinary actions which may be taken.
- Specify the levels of management which have the authority to take the various forms of disciplinary action, ensuring that immediate superiors do not normally have the power to dismiss without reference to senior management.
- Provide for individuals to be informed of the complaints against them and to be given an opportunity to state their case before decisions are reached.
- Give individuals the right to be accompanied by a trade union representative or by a fellow employee of their choice.
- Ensure that except for gross misconduct, no employees are dismissed for a first breach of discipline.
- Ensure that disciplinary action is not taken until the case has been carefully investigated.
- Ensure that individuals are given an explanation for any penalty imposed.
- Provide a right of appeal and specify the procedure to be followed.

Warnings

Paragraph 12 of the Code recommends that in the case of minor offences the following procedure should be used:

Stage 1 — there should be a formal oral warning

Stage 2 — followed by a written warning

Stage 3 — a final written warning

which should make it clear that any recurrence will result in dismissal. However, as the ACAS Advisory Handbook makes clear, this does not mean that three warnings must always be given before dismissal action is taken. On occasion, the seriousness of the offence may make it appropriate to enter the procedure at stage 2 or stage 3. As we shall see below, there are also occasions when dismissal without notice is applicable.

Paragraph 18 of the Code places emphasis on writing and retaining detailed personnel records by the employer who must be able if necessary to provide documentary proof of previous warnings. As a result, a number of employers now adopt the practice of giving written confirmation of an 'oral warning' and of requiring the employee's signature to acknowledge receipt.

The employer's system should include some time limit on warnings, so that after a set period they lapse. *Discipline At Work* offers the following useful advice:

'Normal practice is for different periods for different types of warnings. In general, warnings for minor offences may be valid for up to 6 months, whilst final warnings may remain in force for 12 months or more.

Warnings should cease to be 'live' following the specified period of satisfactory conduct and should be disregarded for future disciplinary purposes. There may however be occasions where an employee's conduct is satisfactory throughout the period the warning is in force only to lapse very soon thereafter.

Where a pattern emerges and there is evidence of abuse, the employee's disciplinary record should be borne in mind in deciding how long any current warning should last. Exceptionally, there may be circumstances where the misconduct is so serious – verging on gross misconduct – that it cannot be realistically disregarded for future disciplinary purposes. In such circumstances it should be made very clear that the final written warning can never be removed and that any recurrence will lead to dismissal.' (page 30)

A warning should be reasonably specific, identifying the precise ground of complaint by the employer. Commentators have suggested that one consequence of this is that a warning on ground 'A' (eg bad language) should not be used as a step in the procedure to dismiss on ground 'B' (eg sub-standard work). This may mean that one employee may be subject to more than one series of warnings at the same time.

In *Auguste Noel Ltd* v *Curtis*, however, we see the EAT taking a different approach in relation to previous warnings concerning un-related misconduct.

Mr Curtis, a 'multi-drop' driver, was dismissed on 18 March 1988 for an act of misconduct involving mishandling company property. In deciding to dismiss him for that offence, the employer took into account two previous written warnings; one dated 16 October 1987 concerning his relationship with other employees and the other, dated 25 February 1988, which referred to unsatisfactory documen-tation and absenteeism.

The EAT held that the industrial tribunal had been wrong to find that the dismissal for mishandling company property was unfair because, in deciding to dismiss for that reason, the employers had taken into account two final written warnings for different offences. Mr Justice Wood stated:

> '. . . it can very rarely be said, if ever, that warnings are irrelevant to the consideration of an employer who is considering dismissal. The mere fact that the conduct was of a different kind on those occasions when warnings were given does not seem to us to render them irrelevant. It is essentially a matter of balance, of doing what is fair and reasonable in the circumstances and the employer is entitled to consider the existence of warnings. He is entitled to look at the substance of the complaint on each of those occasions, how many warnings there have been, the dates and the periods of time between those warnings and indeed all the circumstances of the case.'

Given the relative lack of authority on the point and the fact that the advice in both the ACAS Code No 1 and the Advisory Handbook seems to affirm the basis that warnings are being given for the same reason, it may be that employers are still best advised to keep warnings for different forms of misconduct separate. Of course, there may come a point when the cumulative effect of a number of warnings on different matters provides reasonable grounds to dis-miss. Faced with this sort of situation the employer's final written warning would be on the grounds of generally unacceptable behaviour (see *Industrial Law* by Smith and Wood (4th ed, 1989), page 270).

There are, however, rare occasions where the employee commits a single mistake and the actual or potential consequences of that mistake are so serious that to warn would not be appropriate. This class of case was discussed by the Court of Appeal in **Taylor** v **Alidair Ltd** where it was stated that there are activities in which the degree of professional skill which must be required is so high, and the potential consequences of the smallest departure from that high standard are so serious, that one failure to perform in accordance with those standards is enough to justify dismissal. Examples might be the passenger-carrying airline pilot, the scientist operating the nuclear reactor, the chemist in charge of research into the possible effect of thalidomide, the driver of the Manchester to London express, the driver of an articulated lorry full of sulphuric acid.

Warnings subject to appeal

Where a disciplinary procedure states that a warning is a prerequisite for dismissal, the fact that an appeal against that warning is still pending will be taken into account in deciding whether it is fair or unfair to dismiss in the circumstances, according to the Court of Appeal in **Tower Hamlets Health Authority** v **Anthony**. Lord Justice May gives no detailed guidance on precisely how the reasonable employer is to take account of a pending appeal. But it would appear that the timescale of the appeal may be a relevant factor:

'Where the determination of the appeal will be the day after the dismissal under consideration, it may not be difficult for an Industrial Tribunal to take the view that an employer who dismisses before the determination of an appeal against the necessary formal warning was unreasonable in not waiting that day to see what the determination of the appeal might be. When the timescale is in weeks or in months, circumstances may differ, but the fact of the warning, providing that it is given on adequate evidence and not for any oblique or improper motive, and the fact that it is still subject to an appeal, remain throughout at least two of the circumstances in a case which a reasonable employer and an Industrial Tribunal should take into account.'

Cases of gross misconduct

The ACAS Code of Practice advises that dismissal for a first breach of discipline should be restricted to cases of 'gross misconduct'. This phrase has no statutory definition nor is it defined by the Code of Practice itself, but it is generally regarded as misconduct serious enough to destroy the relationship of trust and confidence between the employer and the employee. This would include:

- theft
- dishonesty
- violence at work
- serious incapability through drink or drugs
- deliberate damage to the employer's property
- serious acts of disobedience to lawful and reasonable orders
- gross negligence causing (or creating the risk of) significant economic loss, damage to property or personal injury.

In other cases, what constitutes gross misconduct may depend on the circumstances and the employer's own disciplinary rules. Employers may codify the orders and requirements for their employees in a series of disciplinary rules. Indeed, EPCA s1(4) requires that the written statement of terms of employment must include 'any disciplinary rules applicable to the employee'. However, the Employment Act 1989 s13 removes the statutory requirement to provide a note of disciplinary rules and appeals procedure where the number of employees of the employer and any associated employer is less than 20. Given that a factor which will be influential in many dismissal cases is whether the employer adequately brought the existence of a particular disciplinary rule to the attention of an employee, small employers would be advised not to take advantage of this exemption.

Disciplinary rules may be regarded as preliminary warnings to employees that the employer regards certain types of offence with particular gravity and that these will be likely to result in instant dismissal (see, for example, *Dalton v Burton's Gold Medal Biscuits*).

However, while it is important that employees should be given a clear indication of the likely sanction consequent upon certain types of misconduct, imposition of that sanction should not be seen as following inexorably once the offence is committed. In other words, there is no such thing as an *automatic* dismissal rule and employers must be prepared to exercise a discretion having allowed the employee to state his or her case and having considered such matters as the seriousness of the infringement of the rule, the employee's length of service and previous disciplinary record.

An illustration is provided by **Ladbroke Racing v Arnott**. The applicants were employed in a betting shop. The employer's disciplinary rules specifically provided that employees were not permitted to place bets or to allow other staff to do so. Two of the applicants had placed such bets, one for a brother on one occasion, and the other occasionally for old-age pensioners. A third applicant, the office manager, had condoned these actions. All three employees were dismissed and an industrial tribunal found the dismissals to be unfair. This decision was upheld by the EAT and the Court of Session on the basis that rules framed in mandatory terms did not leave the employer free from the obligation to act reasonably and to take into account the relatively minor nature of the offences in this particular case.

A final question concerns the situation where an employer summarily dismisses an employee for an offence which is not expressly set out in the disciplinary rules. The answer depends on fact and degree – the more serious the misconduct, the more likely the tribunal will find it reasonable for the employee to have anticipated the employer's reaction.

In *CA Parsons Ltd v McLoughlin*, the dismissal of a shop steward for fighting was upheld, although it was not included in the company's disciplinary rules as gross misconduct. Mr Justice Kilner Brown expressed the view that:

> 'it ought not to be necessary for anybody, let alone a shop steward to have in black and white in the form of a rule that a fight is going to be something that is to be regarded very gravely by management.'

Similarly, in *Ulsterbus v Henderson* the Northern Ireland Court of Appeal rejected a tribunal finding that it was unreasonable to dismiss a bus conductor for failure to give tickets in return for payment, in circumstances where it was not made clear in the disciplinary procedure that offences of this nature would merit the ultimate sanction of dismissal. The Court was of the view that it would be obvious to any employee that failure to give tickets in return for payment was a most serious offence which was likely to lead to dismissal.

Conversely, for offences whose gravity is not so immediately obvious, there will be a requirement for the offence and likely sanction to be clearly expressed in the disciplinary rules, eg consuming alcohol during working hours (***Dairy Produce Packers Ltd* v *Beverstock***) or overstaying leave (***Hoover Ltd* v *Forde***).

It is clearly much better for employers to expressly set out the offences which they regard as sufficiently serious to justify instant dismissal at the outset. Certain employers are reluctant to do this because they believe that this will narrow the scope of their disciplinary powers. In general, however, the courts and tribunals have taken the view that disciplinary rules are not meant to be exhaustive. According to the EAT in ***The Distillers Company (Bottling Services) Ltd* v *Gardner***:

> 'A catalogue of offences which carry the potential sanction of dismissal contained in the company rules may occasionally be useful in assessing the quality of an offence but it does not follow that an offence which does not fall within it can never merit dismissal.'

While it is clear that the employer does not need to list every offence which could lead to dismissal, the offences which *are* listed will be taken as an indication of the character and class of offence which the employer views as gross misconduct. Therefore, a dismissal for an offence of a less serious class or entirely different character than those set out in the disciplinary rules is likely to be regarded as unfair.

A good example of this approach can be seen in ***Dietman* v *London Borough of Brent***. In this case, the Court of Appeal held that the council were not entitled to dismiss the plaintiff social worker summarily without first affording her a hearing under the contractual disciplinary procedure. In any event, on a proper construction of her contract 'gross negligence' did not constitute 'gross misconduct' as defined by the contract which would justify summary dismissal.

The contract defined 'gross misconduct' as 'misconduct of such a nature that the authority is justified in no longer tolerating the continued presence at the place of work of the employee who commits' the offence. Examples were then listed, all of which involved an element of intention on the part of the guilty employee and involved conduct which was either dishonest or disruptive.

The decision emphasises the importance of care in drafting disciplinary procedures and sends the clear message that if employers wish to have the contractual right to be able to dismiss summarily for 'gross negligence', then this should be expressly set out in the disciplinary rules.

Hearings

Paragraph 11 of the ACAS Code of Practice states:

> 'Before a decision is made or a penalty imposed the individual should be interviewed and given the opportunity to state his or her case and should be advised of any rights under the procedure including the right to be represented.'

In **Khanum v Mid-Glamorgan Area Health Authority**, the EAT summarised the three guiding principles of natural justice relating to the conduct of a fair hearing:

1 the employee should know the nature of the allegations made against him or her

2 the employee should be allowed to state his or her case

3 the internal tribunal should act in good faith, ie free from bias.

In **Khanum** it was held that it was not necessary for the conduct of a fair hearing for the employee, a nurse, to be given the opportunity to cross-examine the patients who made complaints against her. A similar approach was adopted by the Northern Ireland Court of Appeal in **Ulsterbus v Henderson** (above) where it was said that it is not incumbent on a reasonable employer to carry out a quasi-judicial investigation with confrontation and cross-examination of witnesses. While some employers might consider this to be necessary or desirable, an employer who fails to do so cannot be said to have acted unreasonably.

While it would appear that an employee may not insist on cross-examination of witnesses, fairness will normally demand that he or she be shown witnesses' statements.

In *Louies* v *Coventry Hood & Seating Co Ltd*, the applicant was dismissed because of his alleged involvement in the theft of company property. Two witnesses had given statements which formed the basis of the company's belief in his guilt. Mr Louies was never shown these statements even though on appeal he asked to see them. An industrial tribunal found that the disciplinary and appeals procedures were unsatisfactory because of the failure of the employers to provide Mr Louies with more than a broad general outline of what the witnesses' statements contained. This made it more difficult for him to answer the charges. The industrial tribunal, however, found that this breach of procedure was not sufficient to persuade it that it invalidated the employer's belief in Mr Louies' guilt.

The EAT allowed the applicant's appeal, stressing the importance of procedural fairness. Mr Justice Wood (President of the EAT) said that where the essence of the case against an employee is contained in written statements by witnesses, it is contrary to natural justice and prima facie unfair for an employer to refuse to let the employee see those statements. There may be the 'delicate situation' of informers where special procedures may have to be used, but these were exceptional cases (see *Linfood Cash & Carry Ltd* v *Thomson*, discussed in chapter 6).

It is a general principle that a person who holds an inquiry must be seen to be impartial, that justice must not only be done but be seen to be done, and that if a reasonable observer with full knowledge of the facts would conclude that the hearing might not be impartial, that is enough. An illustration of an application of these principles is to be found in the decision of the EAT in *Moyes* v *Hylton Castle Working Men's Social Club and Institute Ltd*.

In this case, two witnesses to an alleged act of sexual harassment by a club steward towards a barmaid were also members of the committee which dismissed the steward. The EAT held the dismissal to be unfair on the ground that it was a breach of natural justice for an apparently biased committee to decide the disciplinary matter. In enunciating the general rule that if a person has been a witness he or she should not conduct the inquiry, the EAT did identify certain exceptions, eg the one-person firm.

Subsequently, in **Slater v Leicestershire Health Authority**, the Court of Appeal was at pains to point out that, although as a general principle a person who holds an inquiry must be seen to be impartial, merely because the person conducting a disciplinary hearing had carried out a preliminary investigation did not necessarily mean that he was unable to conduct a fair inquiry. The Court expressed the view that the rules of natural justice did not form an independent ground upon which a decision to dismiss may be attacked, although a breach will clearly become an important matter when the industrial tribunal comes to consider the question of fairness under s57(3).

Appeals

Both the ACAS Code of Practice and Advisory Handbook lay great emphasis on the availability of an appeal from an initial decision to dismiss, and tribunals have held dismissals to be unfair for this reason.

The Handbook advises that an appeals procedure should:

- Specify any time limit within which the appeal should be lodged.
- Provide for appeals to be dealt with speedily, particularly those involving suspension without pay or dismissal.
- Wherever possible, provide for the appeal to be heard by an authority higher than that taking the disciplinary action.
- Spell out the action which may be taken by those hearing the appeal.
- Provide that the employee, or a representative if the employee so wishes, has an opportunity to comment on any new evidence arising during the appeal before any decision is taken.

The Handbook recognises that in small organisations there may be no authority higher than the individual who took the original disciplinary action, and that it is inevitable that they will hear the appeal. In such circumstances, the Handbook's advice is that the appeal hearing 'should be seen as an opportunity to review the original decision in an objective manner and at a quieter time. This can more readily be achieved if some time is allowed to lapse before the appeal hearing' (page 33).

The importance of according the employee a right of appeal was underlined by the House of Lords in **West Midlands Co-operative Society v Tipton**, discussed earlier. Ever since **W Devis & Sons Ltd v Atkins** it was not clear whether, and to what extent, that decision prevented matters arising out of internal appeals from being considered by tribunals as part of their 'reasonableness' assessment under EPCA s57(3). In the **Tipton** case, the House of Lords confirmed that both the denial of a contractual right to appeal and matters arising out of an appeal if one is held can be taken into account by tribunals when they assess the reasonableness of the employer's conduct. Lord Bridge felt that the rule in **Devis** simply prevented conduct unrelated to the real reason for dismissal from affecting the question as to whether an employer acted unreasonably in dismissing the employee for the reason he did. But there was 'nothing in the language of the statute to exclude from consideration . . . evidence relevant to show the strength or weakness of the real reason for dismissal which the employer has the opportunity to consider in the course of an [internal] appeal'.

As a result of the House of Lords' ruling in **Tipton**, in the context of internal appeals, a dismissal will be unfair if:

1   the employer unreasonably treated his or her real reason as a sufficient reason to dismiss the employee – either at the time the original decision to dismiss was made or at the conclusion of an internal appeal *or*

2   the employer refused to entertain an appeal to which the employee was contractually entitled and thereby denied him or her the opportunity to show that in all the circumstances, the real reason for dismissal could not reasonably be treated as sufficient.

The principle set out in **Tipton** concerns a failure to allow the employee a *contractual* right of appeal, but in **National Coal Board v Nash** the EAT was prepared to extend the principle to embrace a failure to permit a non-contractual right of an appeal.

Use of an appeal to remedy earlier procedural flaws

If the appeal amounts to a comprehensive re-hearing of the matter, an industrial tribunal is likely to find a dismissal fair, which would otherwise have been ruled to have been unfair as a result of earlier defects in the disciplinary procedure (*Whitbread & Co plc v Mills*).

Significance of an employee's failure to exercise a right of appeal

According to the EAT in *Chrystie v Rolls Royce (1971) Ltd*, an employee who neglects to appeal against the dismissal under the internal procedure cannot be said to have acquiesced in his or her dismissal. However, failure to exhaust an internal remedy may be of evidential value as an indication of the employee's attitude to the dismissal at the time.

In addition, there is an unresolved conflict as to whether a failure to invoke a right of appeal amounts to a failure to take reasonable steps to mitigate loss, allowing the industrial tribunal to reduce compensation accordingly. (For further details, see *Hoover Ltd v Forde* which favours this approach, and the decision of the Scottish EAT in *William Muir (Bond 9) Ltd v Lamb* which comes out strongly against it.)

Procedural fairness: changes in emphasis

In the early 1970s, the courts and tribunals laid much emphasis on the importance of employers adhering strictly to the basic procedural requirements of fairness, taking the ACAS Code of Practice as their guide. In one of the earliest cases, Sir John Donaldson thought that the only exception to the need for the employee to be allowed to state his or her case was 'where there can be no explanation which could cause the employer to refrain from dismissing the employee' (see *Earl v Slater Wheeler (Airlyne) Ltd*). So it had to be almost inconceivable that the hearing could have made any difference. This test was, however, replaced by more lenient standards.

While the earlier approach could result in a dismissal being found to be unfair on procedural failings alone, later decisions propounded the view that procedural matters were just one of a number of factors to be taken into account (see *Bailey v BP Oil (Kent Refinery) Ltd*).

The highpoint of this dilution of the requirement that the employer should follow a fair procedure is to be found in the test laid down by the EAT in **British Labour Pump Co Ltd v Byrne**. This test allowed the employer to argue that an element of procedural unfairness (such as a failure to give a proper hearing) may be 'forgiven' if the employer can show that, on the balance of probabilities, even if a proper procedure had been complied with the employee would still have been dismissed and the dismissal would then have been fair.

This decision received considerable academic and judicial criticism but was specifically approved of by the Court of Appeal in **W & J Wass Ltd v Binns**. The major criticism of the **British Labour Pump** principle was that it was irreconcilable with the ruling of the House of Lords in **W Devis & Sons Ltd v Atkins**, which held that the employer was not entitled to rely on evidence acquired after dismissal, and that fairness must be judged in the light of facts known to the employer at the time of the dismissal.

This forceful criticism of the logic of **British Labour Pump** has more recently been accepted by the House of Lords in **Polkey v AE Dayton Services**, and the principle has been overruled. This decision is perhaps the most important unfair dismissal decision of the last decade and in the judgements we find a re-emphasis on the importance of following a fair procedure. In the view of Lord Bridge:

'an employer having prima facie grounds to dismiss ... will in the great majority of cases not act reasonably in treating the reason as a sufficient reason for the dismissal unless he has taken steps, conveniently classified in most authorities as 'procedural', which are necessary in the circumstances of the case to justify that course of action.'

Lord Mackay was of the view that what must be considered is what a reasonable employer would have had in mind at the time he or she decided to dismiss:

'If the employer could reasonably have concluded in the light of circumstances known to him at the time of dismissal that consultation or warning would be utterly useless he might well act reasonably even if he did not observe the provisions of the Code.'

It has been argued that there is a significant practical difference between asking whether at the time of the dismissal the employer had reasonable grounds for believing that a fair procedure would have been 'utterly useless' (the new test) and asking whether, in retrospect, it would have made any difference to the outcome (the old test). As a result it is likely that failure to follow a fair procedure may well lead to a finding of unfair dismissal in a much increased proportion of cases.

For those who recognise the value of natural justice in disciplinary procedures the *Polkey* decision will be welcomed along with an earlier ruling of the House of Lords in *West Midlands Co-operative Society* v *Tipton*, discussed earlier.

Representation

The ACAS Code of Practice recommends that employees should have the right to be accompanied by a trade union representative or fellow employee of their choice. Employees should be informed of this right on being invited to attend the disciplinary interview and a refusal to allow representation may well result in a finding of unfair dismissal (*Rank Xerox (UK) Ltd* v *Goodchild*).

The case law would tend to suggest that there is no *general* right to legal representation at internal disciplinary hearings (*Sharma* v *British Gas Corporation*. However, there may be situations in which it is appropriate for a solicitor to be present, eg where criminal proceedings are pending.

Given the potential damage to industrial relations where management propose to discipline a trade union official, the Code recommends that no action beyond an oral warning should be taken until the case has been discussed with a senior trade union representative or full-time official.

6 THE PROBLEM AREAS OF DISMISSAL

In this chapter, the scope of the five categories of admissible reasons for dismissal is discussed. These five categories are as follows:

- capability/qualifications
- conduct
- redundancy
- continued employment involving breach of the law
- some other substantial reason.

In the course of this discussion particular reference will be made to the guidance provided by the courts and tribunals in relation to a number of frequently recurring dismissal issues. These are as follows:

- sub-standard performance
- absence (long-term illness, persistent absenteeism)
- dishonesty
- redundancy
- business reorganisation dismissals.

Capability/qualifications

Under this head the employer has to show that the reason (or, if there was more than one, the principal reason) for the dismissal 'related to the capability or qualifications of the employee for performing work of the kind which he was employed to do' (EPCA s57(2)(a)).

'Capability' is defined in s57(4) as 'capability assessed by reference to skill, aptitude, health or any other physical or mental quality', and 'qualifications' as 'any degree, diploma or other academic, technical or professional qualification relevant to the position which the employee held'.

'Qualifications' has to be construed in the light of the particular position which the employee held. Therefore, in certain circumstances, failure to pass a required aptitude test can be a reason for dismissal relating to qualification to do the job (*Blackman* v *The Post Office*). However, a mere licence, permit or authorisation is not a qualification unless it is substantially concerned with the employee's aptitude or ability to do the job (*Blue Star Ship Management Ltd* v *Williams*).

Typically, in cases where the employee's capability is at issue, two major human resource management problems are often considered – sub-standard work and absenteeism because of ill health. These aspects will be examined below.

Sub-standard work

Sub-standard work may occur for a variety of reasons. It has been suggested that it is only when the employee is inherently incapable of reasonable standards of work that the dismissal is related to 'capability' within EPCA s57(2)(a). Where the employee has the capacity to do the job but produces poor performance because of carelessness or lack of motivation, then the matter is probably better dealt with as misconduct (*Sutton & Gates (Luton) Ltd* v *Boxall*).

Evidence of incompetence

'Wherever a man is dismissed for incapacity or incompetence it is sufficient that the employer honestly believes on reasonable grounds that the man is incapable or incompetent. It is not necessary for the employer to prove that he is in fact incapable or incompetent' (Lord Denning in *Taylor* v *Alidair Ltd*).

Therefore, the test as to whether an employee is incompetent is not purely subjective, and the requirement of reasonable grounds dictates that the employer should have carried out a proper and full investigation into the question. However, as the above quote from Lord Denning suggests, the employer is not required to *prove* that the employee was in fact incompetent. In this sense, the test resembles the approach adopted in relation to suspected misconduct, eg suspicion of dishonesty, discussed later in this chapter.

In assessing incompetence, the courts and tribunals have shown themselves prepared to give considerable weight to the employer's opinions and views concerning incapacity. For example, in **Cook v Thomas Linnell & Sons Ltd**, the EAT expressed the view that although employers must act reasonably when removing from a particular post an employee whom they consider to be unsatisfactory, it was important that the unfair dismissal legislation did not impede employers unreasonably in the efficient management of their business. The EAT went on to state:

> 'When responsible employers have genuinely come to the conclusion over a reasonable period of time that a manager is incompetent we think that it is some evidence that he is incompetent.'

General poor performance

The ACAS Advisory Handbook offers the following valuable guidance to employers who may be faced with a case of poor performance:

- the employee should be asked for an explanation and the explanation checked
- where the reason is the lack of the required skills, the employee should, wherever practicable, be assisted through training and given reasonable time to reach the required standard of performance
- where despite encouragement and assistance the employee is unable to reach the required standard of performance, consideration should be given to finding suitable alternative work
- where alternative work is not available, the position should be explained to the employee before dismissal action is taken
- an employee should not normally be dismissed because of poor performance unless warnings and a chance to improve have been given
- if the main cause of poor performance is the changing nature of the job, employers should consider whether the situation may properly be treated as redundancy rather than a capability issue.

Long-term sickness absence

One of the most common and difficult problems facing employers and trade union representatives in the realm of disciplinary practice and procedure is employee absence through sickness or injury. In these situations the employer will frequently have to resolve a conflict between pressing economic considerations and the employee's claim for job security and fair treatment where he or she is absent through no fault of his or her own. Likewise, trade union representatives must protect those members who, in addition to shouldering the burden of ill health, face the prospect of unemployment.

In cases of exceptionally severe and incapacitating illness where it is highly unlikely that the employee will ever be fit to return to work, the contract may be regarded as *frustrated* and, therefore, terminated by operation of law rather than dismissal. The rules governing the doctrine of frustration and its relationship to long-term sickness absence and imprisonment are discussed in chapter 2.

Given that the frustration doctrine offers employers a convenient way in which to avoid the unfair dismissal provisions, the courts are generally reluctant to apply it to contracts which are terminable by notice. Therefore, in less drastic cases of long-term sickness absence, a body of case law has developed on the question of the fairness of a dismissal in such circumstances.

While the rules as to reasonableness discussed in chapter 5 apply to dismissals for ill health, industrial tribunals have also, in considering whether an employer acted reasonably, taken into account:

1   the circumstances of the particular case *and*

2   what procedures have been followed by the employer in making the decision to dismiss.

Circumstances of the dismissal

The substantive aspect of the tribunal's inquiry revolves around the question of whether it was reasonable of the employer to dismiss in the circumstances of the particular circumstances of the case. In **Spencer** v **Paragon Wallpapers Ltd**, Mr Justice Phillips set out the relevant consideration as follows:

'The nature of the illness, the likely length of the continuing absence, the need for the employers to have done the work which the employee was employed to do ... The basic question which has to be determined in every case is whether, in all the circumstances, the employer can be expected to wait any longer and, if so, how much longer? Every case will be different, depending on the circumstances.'

Therefore, a balance has to be struck between job security and the interests of the business (see para 40 of the *Industrial Relations Code of Practice* 1972). Where the absent employee holds a position which cannot be filled easily on a temporary basis and his or her continued absence is inconsistent with the operational efficiency of the undertaking, tribunals have held dismissals to be fair (see *Tan v Berry Bros and Rudd Ltd* and *McPhee v George H Wright*).

The question of the time the employee must be away from work before it may be reasonable for an employer to dismiss him or her depends, as was stated in *Spencer*, on the circumstances of each case. A significant factor may be the size of the employer's undertaking. In a large firm, the disruption caused by sickness absence may be minimal, but in a small business such absences may be extremely serious.

Where an employee is covered by a contractual sick pay scheme can the employer dismiss before the sick pay entitlement elapses? It may be assumed that if an employer has contracted to provide a certain period of sick pay it would not normally be reasonable to dismiss before this time span has elapsed. However, this does not mean that it will always be unfair to dismiss during the currency of a sick pay period.

In *Coulson v Felixstowe Dock and Railway Co*, the company dismissed an employee whose lengthy absence over the previous two years had caused inconvenience from time to time when, because of a labour shortage, a replacement could not be found. He sought to argue before the industrial tribunal that he should not have been dismissed before his sick pay entitlement was exhausted. This contention was rejected by the tribunal which found that the sick pay scheme was 'a financial provision and not a provision which in any event indicates the amount of absence to which an employee is entitled, if he is sick'.

In line with this approach, merely because the absent employee has exhausted his or her sick pay entitlement does not mean that an employer can automatically dismiss the employee even where the contract so provides. In *Hardwick* v *Leeds Area Health Authority*, the tribunal stated:

> 'It seems to us to be quite outmoded at the present day for a rule to exist that employees on exhaustion of sick pay should be automatically dismissed irrespective of the circumstances as if it was one of the laws of the Medes and Persians and it is not a reasonable one to apply.'

Adequacy of procedures before dismissal

A dismissal will be found to be unfair if the employer has failed to follow adequate procedures in coming to the conclusion that the dismissal was necessary. An employer will be expected to make a reasonable effort to inform him or herself of the true medical position, and this will normally entail consulting the employee and seeking, with the employee's consent, a medical opinion. A model letter of inquiry to an employee's general practitioner, approved by the British Medical Association, is included as Appendix 4 (vii) to the ACAS Advisory Handbook.

The Access to Medical Reports Act 1988, which came into force on 1 January 1989, now regulates the supply of medical reports on employees to employers. The Act obliges an employer to inform an employee of its intention to ask the employee's doctor for a medical report and to obtain the employee's consent. There is also a requirement that the employee be informed of the following rights under the Act:

- the right to refuse consent
- the right of access to the report both before and after it is supplied to the employer
- the right to refuse consent to the report being supplied to the employer
- the right to amend the report where it is considered by the employee to be 'incorrect and misleading'.

The right to amend is qualified by the fact that the Act allows the doctor to accept or reject the amendments. However, where the doctor does not accept the patient's amendments, he or she must attach a statement of the patient's views to the report (s5(2)(b)).

If an employee does refuse to give consent to allow the employer to approach his or her doctor, it may be taken by the tribunal to confirm the employer's feeling that the employee is unfit to carry out his or her duties (see *Leeves* v *Edward Hope Ltd*).

Many employers now make it a term of employment that the employee agrees, if and when requested, to undergo a medical examination by the organisation's own occupational health practitioner or by an independent doctor to be nominated by the employer. The provisions of the Access to Medical Reports Act 1988 only apply to reports requested from the employee's *own* doctor.

The decision whether to dismiss is a managerial one rather than a medical one and, therefore, the medical opinion which the employer seeks must be sufficiently detailed to allow him or her to make a rational and informed decision (*East Lindsey District Council* v *Daubney*). In the event of a conflict of opinion, some tribunal decisions have favoured the opinion of the employer's own medical officer over that of the employee's own doctor on the basis that the former is more aware of the demands of the job (see *Jeffries* v *BP Tanker Co Ltd*).

The need for consultation with the employee was stressed in *Spencer* v *Paragon Wallpapers Ltd* (above) and strongly affirmed by the EAT's decision in *East Lindsey District Council* v *Daubney* (above). However, consultation has not always been required by industrial tribunals. In *Taylorplan Catering (Scotland) Ltd* v *McInally*, it was suggested that where a tribunal finds that the circumstances were such that a consultation would have made no difference to the result, lack of consultation could be justified.

In this case, the EAT was of the view that the guidelines in *British Labour Pump* could be applied in cases involving ill health. With the rejection of those guidelines by the House of Lords in *Polkey* it is likely that consultation will be required in the vast majority of cases.

Assuming that the industrial tribunal is satisfied that the employers could not be expected to wait any longer before replacing the sick employee, and that they have made reasonable efforts to establish the true medical position, the employers may find that they have one further requirement to comply with before they can successfully defend a claim of unfair dismissal – an obligation to look for alternative work for the sick employee within the organisation. Where there is a suitable job in existence which the employee is capable of performing, a failure to offer it to the employee may well cast doubt upon the fairness of the dismissal.

Therefore, if there is an existing job, even if it is lower paid, the employer should offer the alternative work to the employee. If the employee refuses any such offers, then it seems reasonable for the employer to dismiss the employee. This statement requires some qualification in the sense that the employer is only required to consider the employee's ability to perform existing jobs – there is no duty on the employer to create a new job (see **Merseyside and North Wales Electricity Board v Taylor**).

However, the employer may be expected to go to reasonable lengths to modify a particular job in order to meet the employee's needs (see **Carricks (Caterers) Ltd v Nolan** in which an employer was held to be unreasonable in not offering alternative work to an employee who was no longer fit to do shift work but could have coped with a day job).

For a checklist on handling long-term sickness absence, see page 42 of the ACAS Advisory Handbook, *Discipline At Work*.

Persistent absenteeism

While long-term absence is treated as a matter relating to capability, it is clear that persistent absenteeism should be regarded as a matter of misconduct and can be dealt with under the ordinary disciplinary procedure.

In **International Sports Ltd v Thomson**, the applicant's attendance record had badly deteriorated to a level of 25 per cent for the last 18 months of her employment. Most of these absences were covered by medical certificates and were concerned with a variety of ailments such as dizzy spells, anxiety and nerves, bronchitis, virus infection, cystitis, dyspepsia and flatulence.

Ms Thomson's degree of absence was well above the acceptable level of 8 per cent which had been agreed with the union and therefore, within the terms of the agreed disciplinary procedure, she was warned on several occasions about her absenteeism. A final written warning informed her that if her attendance did not improve then dismissal could result. However, her attendance record did not improve and she was summarily dismissed. The industrial tribunal found the dismissal unfair on the grounds that the employers had not engaged in the process of investigation and consultation required in a case concerning the capability of an employee as a result of ill health.

The EAT allowed the employer's appeal and stated that the guidelines set out in *Spencer* and *Daubney* were not relevant when considering the 'impact of an unacceptable level of intermittent absences due to unconnected minor ailments'. According to the EAT this type of situation comes under the heading of dismissal for conduct (EPCA s57(2)(b) or possibly some other substantial reason (EPCA s57(1)(b)) rather than capability. Therefore, the use of warnings was an appropriate means of dealing with the problem:

> 'In such a case, it would be placing too heavy a burden on the employer to require him to carry out a formal medical investigation and, even if he did, such an investigation would rarely be fruitful because of the transient nature of the employee's symptoms and complaints. What is required, in our judgement is, firstly, that there should be a fair review by the employer of the attendance records and the reasons for it; and, secondly, appropriate warnings after the employee has been given an opportunity to make representations. If there is no adequate improvement in the attendance record, it is likely that in most cases the employer will be justified in treating the persistent absences as a sufficient reason for dismissing the employee.'

This approach to persistent absenteeism was reinforced by the important decision of the EAT in *Rolls Royce* v *Walpole*. In this case, the employee's average absence over the last three years of his employment was approximately 50 per cent. The industrial tribunal found that his dismissal was unfair on the grounds that the company should have obtained a more up to date medical report from its own doctor or have given the employee an opportunity of providing medical evidence of his own.

On appeal by the employers, the EAT emphasised that a further medical examination could not have been of any help because it had never been suggested that the applicant was suffering from any underlying condition rendering him more susceptible to illness than his fellow employees. Thus, given that the applicant had received sufficient warning and the company's grievance procedures had been followed meticulously, the majority of the EAT were satisfied that the decision to dismiss the employee 'was well within the range of responses which reasonable employers could have taken having regard to equity and substantial merits of the case, in treating the employee's poor attendance record after warning as a sufficient reason for dismissing him'.

A checklist offering valuable guidance on handling frequent and persistent short-term absence is contained in the ACAS Handbook, *Dismissal at Work* on page 41. The Handbook advises that:

- Absences should be investigated promptly and the employee asked to give an explanation.
- Where there is no medical advice to support frequent self-certificated medical absences, the employee should be asked to consult a doctor to establish whether medical treatment is necessary and whether the underlying reasons for absence is work-related.
- If after investigation it appears that there were no good reasons for the absences, the matter should be dealt with under the disciplinary procedure.
- Where absences arise from temporary domestic problems, the employer in deciding appropriate action should consider whether an improvement in attendance is likely.
- In all cases the employee should be told what improvement in attendance is expected and warned of the likely consequence if this does not happen.
- If there is no improvement, the employee's age, length of service, performance, the likelihood of a change in attendance, the availability of suitable alternative work and the effect of past and future absences on the business should all be taken into account in deciding appropriate action.

The malingering employee

Where the employer suspects that the absent employee is malingering, the issue should be treated as a matter of misconduct and normal disciplinary procedures followed. In **Hutchinson v Enfield Rolling Mills Ltd**, the employee was off sick but travelled to Brighton in order to participate in a union demonstration. It was held that a doctor's medical certificate was not conclusive proof of genuine sickness absence if the employer had other evidence that the employee was fit enough to attend work. This principle would, of course, apply with even more force where the employee has self-certificated absence.

Conduct

Dismissal for a reason related to the conduct of the employer covers a multitude of sins encompassing those capable of amounting to gross misconduct:

- violence
- theft
- a serious act of disobedience
- gross negligence

  and also less serious infringements of discipline such as:

- minor acts of insubordination
- bad language
- bad timekeeping.

As we have seen, except in cases of dismissal for a single act of gross misconduct, the courts and tribunals expect employers to adopt the system of warnings discussed in chapter 5.

The commission, or alleged commission, of a criminal offence by the employee is the form of misconduct which has generated the most case law and difficulty. For this reason, particular attention will be given to this area.

Dishonesty and other criminal offences

The courts and tribunals maintain a distinction between offences committed at work and those outside. Whether the commission of a criminal offence outside work merits an employee's dismissal depends above all on its relevance to the individual's duties as an employee. Tribunals take into account the following matters:

- the status of the employee
- the nature of the offence
- the employee's past record
- the employee's access to cash (in cases of dishonesty)
- proximity to members of the public (in cases of offences of violence).

Furthermore, where the alleged offence is committed outside employment, the ACAS Code of Practice advises that employees should not be dismissed 'solely because a charge against them is pending or because they are absent through having been remanded in custody' (para 15(c)).

Nevertheless, there may be cases where the period of absence on remand is lengthy and the employer may be justified, in the interests of the business, in seeking a permanent replacement (see *Kingston* v *British Railways Board*). Indeed, a lengthy period in custody on remand or a sentence of imprisonment on conviction may result in a finding that the employment contract has been 'frustrated', as we saw in chapter 2.

An employee may be fairly dismissed where he or she conceals from his or her employer a criminal conviction imposed before the employment began and which is not a 'spent' conviction under the provisions of the Rehabilitation Of Offenders Act 1974. Whether or not a conviction is spent and the individual is a 'rehabilitated person' under the Act depends upon the severity of the sentence and the time which has elapsed since it was imposed. A sentence of life imprisonment or a sentence exceeding 30 months is never spent. The following table offers some guidance on when a particular conviction becomes spent.

Sentence	Rehabilitation period
Imprisonment for more than six months but less than 30 months	10 years
Imprisonment for a term under six months' duration	7 years
Borstal training	7 years
A fine or other sentence not expressly covered by the Act	5 years

Section 4(3) of the Act makes it automatically unfair to dismiss someone on the grounds of a conviction which is spent or because of failure to disclose it (see *Property Guards Ltd* v *Taylor and Kershaw*).

The scope of this provision is limited by subsequent regulations which exclude certain professions and employments from the Act. Exempted groups include:

- medical practitioners
- lawyers
- accountants
- veterinary surgeons
- dentists
- nurses
- opticians
- pharmaceutical chemists
- judicial appointments
- justices' clerks
- probation officers
- those employed by local authorities in connection with the provision of social services
- those offices and employments concerned with the provisions of services, schooling, training, etc to persons under the age of 18 where the holder will have access to young persons (or employment on premises used for providing such services).

See the Rehabilitation of Offenders Act 1974 (Exceptions) Order 1975 (SI 1975 No 1023) as amended by the Rehabilitation of Offenders Act 1974 (Exceptions) (Amendment) Orders 1986 (SI 1986 No 1249 and SI 1986 No 2268).

An employer, when recruiting to an exempted occupation, should inform candidates in writing that spent convictions must be disclosed. If a person is employed having failed to disclose a conviction, the employer may be held to have acted fairly if he or she dismisses on subsequent discovery of the conviction (see *Torr* v *British Railways Board*).

Suspected dishonesty within employment

As in all cases of misconduct, employers should not dismiss for dishonesty unless and until they have formed a genuine and reasonable belief in the guilt of the employee. The authoritative guidance on this issue is *British Home Stores* v *Burchell* (approved by the Court of Appeal in *W Weddel & Co Ltd* v *Tepper*). The test formulated by the EAT in *Burchell* is whether the employer:

1   entertained a reasonable belief in the guilt of the employee

2   had reasonable grounds for that belief *and*

3   had carried out as much investigation into the matter as was reasonable.

What if the criminal court subsequently acquits a dismissed person? Remember that the employer is judged on the reasonableness of his or her actions *at the time of the dismissal* and not on the basis of what happens afterwards. Therefore, as long as the *Burchell* tests are satisfied then such a dismissal will be likely to be held to be fair. The standard of proof required in an unfair dismissal case (on the balance of probabilities) is not as onerous as in a criminal case (beyond all reasonable doubt). In *Post Office Counters Ltd* v *Heavey*, the EAT reminded tribunals that when considering case law containing guidelines on the application of EPCA s57(3), it was important for them to bear in mind that the burden of proof was made neutral by the amendments made to that section by the Employment Act 1980. So, cases such as *British Home Stores* v *Burchell* and *Weddel* v

Tepper are examining the old law, which placed the burden on the employer, rather than balancing that burden of proof between employer and employee in accordance with the amended s57(3).

A reasonable investigation

What constitutes reasonable investigation will very much depend on the circumstances of the particular case. At one extreme there is the employee who is caught 'red-handed', while at the other the guilt of the employee may be a matter of pure inference. The closer the case is to the latter end of the continuum, the more exacting the standard of inquiry and investigation required.

In cases where the position is less than clear-cut, it is clearly advisable for the employer to carry out an investigation *before* putting the accusation to the employee. This is because an accusation without reasonable foundation could entitle the accused employee to resign and claim constructive dismissal (see *Robinson* v *Crompton Parkinson Ltd*).

Where an employee, having been charged with or convicted of a criminal offence, refuses to co-operate with the employer's investigation, this should not prevent the employer from proceeding. In *Carr* v *Alexander Russell Ltd*, it was suggested that it would be improper, after an employee has been arrested and charged with a criminal offence alleged to have been committed in the course of employment, for the employer to seek to question the employee.

However, this approach was rejected in *Harris (Ipswich) Ltd* v *Harrison*, where the view was expressed that there was nothing to prevent an employer in such circumstances from discussing the matter with the employee or his or her representative. What needs to be discussed is not so much the alleged offence as the action the employer is proposing to take, and whether there are any mitigating circumstances such as a lengthy and previously unblemished service record.

Therefore, where an employee – perhaps after having taken legal advice – chooses to remain silent, he or she should be given written warning that, unless he or she provides further information, a disciplinary decision will be taken on the basis of the information that is available and could result in dismissal (see *Harris and Shepherd* v *Courage (Eastern) Ltd*).

The ACAS Handbook, *Discipline At Work*, advises that where the police are involved they should not be asked to conduct the investigation on behalf of the employer, nor should they be present at any disciplinary hearing or interview (see page 37 of the Handbook). Similarly, the employer cannot simply leave the disciplinary decision to the criminal justice system – deciding not to carry out an internal investigation but to automatically dismiss the employee if he or she is found guilty at trial (see *McLaren* v *National Coal Board*).

Dealing with information from an informant

We saw in chapter 5 that, while it would appear that the employee has no right to cross-examine witnesses, there is an obligation to make available to the employee any written statements of witnesses. Employers are confronted with a particularly difficult problem where they are provided with information by a person who does not wish his or her identity to be disclosed. A careful balance must be maintained between the desirability to protect informants who may be genuinely in fear of reprisal, and providing a fair hearing for the employee accused of misconduct. In *Linfood Cash & Carry Ltd* v *Thomson*, the EAT offered the following valuable guidance to employers where allegations concerning an employee's conduct are made by an informant:

1   The information given by the informant should be reduced into writing in one or more statements. Initially these statements should be taken without regard to the fact that in those cases where anonymity is to be preserved, it may subsequently prove to be necessary to omit or erase certain parts of the statements before submission to others, in order to prevent identification.

2   In taking statements, the following should be regarded as important:

- Date, time and place of each or any observation or incident.
- The opportunity and ability to observe clearly and with accuracy.
- The circumstantial evidence, such as knowledge of a system or arrangement or the reason for the presence of the informer, and why certain small details are memorable.
- Whether the informant has suffered at the hands of the accused or has any other reason to fabricate the allegation, whether from personal grudge or any other reason or principle.

3   Further investigation can then take place either to confirm or undermine the information given. Corroboration is clearly desirable.

4   Tactful inquiries into the character and background of the informant may well be thought suitable and advisable as well as any other information which may tend to add or detract from the value of the informant's statement.

5   If the informant is prepared to attend a disciplinary hearing no problem will arise but if, as in *Linfood Cash & Carry Ltd* v *Thomson*, the employer is satisfied that the fear of reprisal is genuine, then a decision will need to be made whether or not to continue with the disciplinary process.

6   If the disciplinary process is to continue, it is desirable that at each stage of the procedure, the member of management responsible for that hearing should interview the informant and satisfy him or herself that weight is to be given to the information.

7   The written statement of the informant, if necessary with omissions to avoid identification, should be made available to the employee and his or her representatives.

8   If the employee or his or her representative raises any particular and relevant issue which should be put to the informant, it may be desirable to adjourn for the Chair of the disciplinary hearing to make further inquiries of the informant.

9   Although it is always desirable for notes to be taken during disciplinary procedures, it is particularly important in cases where an informant is involved that full and careful notes be taken.

10 While not peculiar to cases where informants have been the cause for the initiation of an investigation, it is important that if evidence from an investigating officer is to be taken at a hearing, it should where possible be prepared in a written form.

'Blanket' dismissals

The general rule is that employers may only dismiss for misconduct if they entertain a genuine and reasonable belief in the employee's guilt (see *British Home Stores* v *Burchell* (above)). This rule was modified in cases where, despite all reasonable investigations, the employer is unable to identify the culprit, but knows it must be one of two employees. In such a case the Court of Appeal has held that it is reasonable to dismiss both (see *Monie* v *Coral Racing Ltd*).

This principle concerning 'blanket' dismissals has recently been extended by the EAT to cases relating to the conduct or capability of the employee where no dishonesty is involved (see *Whitbread & Co plc* v *Thomas*). According to this case, an employer who cannot identify which member of a group was responsible for an act can fairly dismiss the whole group, even where it is probable that not all were guilty of the act, *provided three conditions are satisfied*:

1 The act in question must be such that, if committed by an identified individual, it would justify dismissal of that individual.

2 The tribunal must be satisfied that the act was committed by one or more of the group, all of whom can be shown to be individually capable of having committed the act complained of.

3 The tribunal must be satisfied that there has been a proper investigation by the employer to identify the person or persons responsible for the act.

This principle has been most recently applied by the EAT in *Parr* v *Whitbread plc*. Mr Parr was employed as a branch manager of one of the respondent's off-licence shops. He was dismissed along with three other employees when the sum of £4,600 was stolen from the shop, in circumstances which indicated that it was an inside job. Each of the four had equal opportunity of committing the theft and the employers found it impossible to ascertain which of them was actually guilty. The EAT upheld the industrial tribunal's finding of a fair dismissal.

Unfair redundancy dismissals

Redundancy is a prima facie fair ground for dismissal (EPCA s57(1) and (2)). It is important to note, however, that the statutory presumption that a dismissal is for redundancy under EPCA s91(2) which applies when the claim is for a redundancy payment, does not apply in relation to an unfair dismissal claim. Therefore, it is up to the employer to prove that redundancy was the reason for dismissal.

Even where the employer has succeeded in this task, the dismissal for redundancy may still be attacked as unfair on one of three grounds:

1   Selection for redundancy for a reason 'specified in s58(1)', ie trade union membership or activity or non-membership (EPCA s59(a)).

2   Selection for redundancy in contravention of a customary arrangement or agreed procedure relating to redundancy where there were no 'special reasons' justifying departure from that arrangement or procedure in the circumstances of the particular case (EPCA s59(b)).

This provision, as with s59(a), is subject to the proviso that another employee holding a similar position as the one selected for redundancy has been retained, although the circumstances constituting redundancy applied equally to that employee. The most common basis for selection under a redundancy agreement is 'last in, first out', but may also allow other criteria to be taken into account such as skill, competence, attendance and disciplinary records.

3   Unreasonable redundancy under EPCA s57(3). While it is an automatically unfair dismissal not to comply with a redundancy agreement or arrangement, it does not follow that it is necessarily fair to follow it.

Under s57(3), the industrial tribunal still has to decide whether an employer's selection of a particular employee for redundancy was reasonable (see *NC Watling & Co Ltd* v *Richardson*). Also, certain types of selection agreements, such as 'part-timers first', may amount to indirect sex discrimination (see *Clarke and Powell* v *Eley (IMI) Kynoch Ltd* and compare with *Kidd* v *DRG Ltd (UK)*).

Whether or not there is a redundancy agreement, the employee may challenge the fairness of the redundancy dismissal under s57(3) (this was laid down by the Court of Appeal in *Bessenden Properties Ltd* v *Corness*).

The leading case is *Williams* v *Compair Maxam Ltd*, where the EAT laid down five principles of 'good industrial relations practice' which should generally be followed in redundancies where the employees are represented by an independent and recognised trade union. These guidelines were as follows:

1   To give as much warning as possible.

2   To consult with the union, particularly relating to the criteria to be applied in selection for redundancy.

(Guidelines 1 and 2 reflect the provisions of the Employment Protection Act 1975 ss99-107 which oblige employers to consult recognised unions 'at the earliest opportunity'. If the employer is proposing to dismiss 100 or more employees at one establishment over a 90 day period, consultations must commence not less than 90 days before the first dismissal. If it is proposed to dismiss 10 or more over a 30 day period, consultations should take place not less than 30 days before the first dismissal takes effect. There is no minimum period where the employer proposes to dismiss less than 10 employees. An employee who suffers loss by the lack of consultation may receive compensation in the form of a 'protective award'.)

3   To adopt objective rather than subjective criteria for selection, eg experience, length of service, attendance, etc.

4   To select in accordance with the criteria, considering any representations made by the union regarding selection.

5   To consider the possibility of redeployment rather than dismissal.

These guidelines have since been approved and applied by the Northern Ireland Court of Appeal in *Robinson* v *Carrickfergus BC*, while in *Grundy (Teddington) Ltd* v *Plummer and Salt*, the EAT emphasised that the guidelines should be applied flexibly, as one or more of the five points may not be appropriate in the particular circumstances of the case.

While the EAT in England has been in favour of a flexible but general application of the *Compair Maxam* guidelines, this approach has not found favour North of the Border. In *A Simpson & Son (Motors) Ltd v Reid and Findlater*, Lord MacDermott felt that the guidelines had been misapplied by the tribunals and that they only had application in situations where there was an independent recognised trade union. He was of the view that the guidelines had no relevance in a situation, such as that before the court, of a small business faced with a selection of two out of three people where no trade union was involved. In *Meikle v McPhail (Charleston Arms)*, Lord MacDonald, referring somewhat despairingly to the 'so-called principles' set out in *Compair Maxam*, said:

> 'These principles must primarily refer to large organisations in which a significant number of redundancies are contemplated. In our view they should be applied with caution to circumstances such as the present where the size and administrative resources of the employer are minimal.' (See also *Buchanan v Tilcon Ltd*.)

A decision is awaited from the Court of Appeal as to whether it approves of the *Compair Maxam* guidelines or adopts the restrictive Scottish approach. If the latter view was adopted, then the law would return to a pre-*Compair Maxam* state of affairs, which rarely challenged management's approach to redundancy.

Strong implicit support for the need for the *Compair Maxam* guidelines, however, may now be derived from the House of Lords' decision in *Polkey v AE Dayton Services Ltd*, which was discussed in chapter 5. This decision rejected the so-called 'no difference rule' – ie the rule that an unfair procedure leading to a dismissal does not render the dismissal unfair if it made no difference to the outcome. In the course of his judgement, Lord Bridge, while not referring to the *Compair Maxam* case by name, stated:

> '. . . in the case of redundancy, the employer will not normally be acting reasonably unless he warns and consults any employees affected or their representative, adopts a fair basis on which to select for redundancy and takes such steps as may be reasonable to avoid or minimise redundancy by redeployment within his own organisation.'

Lord Bridge was of the view that if an industrial tribunal felt it likely the employee would have been dismissed even if consultation had taken place, the compensation could be reduced by 'a percentage representing the chance that the employee would still have lost his employment'. This was a better approach than the 'all or nothing' decision which resulted from the application of the 'no difference rule'. Moreover, Lord Bridge stated that:

'In a case where an Industrial Tribunal held that dismissal on the ground of redundancy would have been inevitable at the time it took place, even if the appropriate procedural steps had been taken, I do not, as presently advised, think this would necessarily preclude a discretionary order for re-engagement on suitable terms, if the altered circumstances considered by the Tribunal at the date of the hearing were thought to justify it.'

For further discussion of redundancy dismissals see the book by Sue Morris in this Employment Law Guide series, *Handling Redundancy.*

Dismissal to avoid breach of a statutory duty or restriction

It is potentially fair for an employer to dismiss an employee because the employee 'could not continue to work in the position which he held without contravention (either on his part or on that of his employer) of a duty or restriction imposed by or under an enactment' (EPCA s57(2)(d)).

Before proposing to dismiss on this basis, the employer should seek legal advice as to whether the continued employment of the employee *would involve a breach of the law.* The courts and tribunals have taken a particularly strict view of the scope of the sub-section and have held that it does not apply where the employer genuinely but mistakenly believes that continued employment would be unlawful. For example, in **Bouchaala v Trusthouse Forte Hotels Ltd** the company dismissed the employee after being wrongly informed by the Department of Employment that he would not qualify for a work permit and that his continued employment would be unlawful. The dismissal was held not to fall into s57(2)(d) but was held to be fair under s57(1)(b) – some other substantial reason.

The fact that the employer could not have lawfully continued to employ an employee without contravening the law does not inevitably lead to the conclusion that a dismissal falling within s57(2)(d) is fair. In other words, the tribunal still has to be satisfied that the employer behaved reasonably within s57(3) (***Sandhu v (1) Department of Education and Science (2) London Borough of Hillingdon***).

In practical terms, very few cases arise under this heading. The most common examples are cases where the individual employee is employed as a driver and then is disqualified from driving. In this sort of situation the employer should consider whether there is alternative work which can be offered to the disqualified driver before turning to dismissal (***Fearn v Tayford Motor Company Ltd***).

Some other substantial reason

This is a 'catch-all' category set out in EPCA s57(1)(b) and is intended to cover situations not encompassed by the four explicit admissible reasons (***R S Components Ltd v Irwin***). As with the other admissible reasons, the burden of proof is on the employer and if it cannot be shown that the reason which motivated the employer to dismiss was 'substantial', then the tribunal will find for the applicant.

Examples of dismissals which have been held to fall within this general residual category are as follows:

1 Non-renewal of a fixed term contract where it can be shown that there was a genuine need for fixed term employment and the temporary nature of the employment was made known to the employee at the outset (see ***Terry v East Sussex County Council*** and ***North Yorkshire County Council v Fay***).

2 Dismissal of temporary replacements. In two cases, statute provides that the dismissal of temporary replacement staff will constitute 'some other substantial reason'.

The first is in respect of the dismissal of the replacement of an employee who has been on maternity leave (EPCA s61(1)) and the second concerns the dismissal of an individual employed to cover the absence of an employee who is suspended on medical grounds under EPCA s19 (EPCA s61 (2)). Such dismissals will be potentially justifiable provided that the replacements have been informed in writing at the time of their engagement that their employment would be terminated on the return to work of the permanent employee. The tribunal must also be satisfied that it was reasonable to dismiss and a relevant factor may be whether the employer has considered the availability of alternative work for the replacement employee.

3 Customer pressure to dismiss. Dismissal of an employee because an important customer of the employer was not willing to accept that employee doing their work, has been held to constitute a substantial reason for dismissal (*Scott Packing & Warehousing Co Ltd* v *Paterson*).

However, if the employer wishes to rely on this ground for dismissal, clear evidence must be produced that the valued customer had threatened to withdraw custom unless the employee was dismissed (*Grootcon (UK) Ltd* v *Keld*).

In addition, before finally acceding to the demand, the employer should investigate the matter thoroughly in consultation with the customer and the employee, considering the possibility of deploying the employee on alternative work if it is available (*Dobie* v *Burns International Security Services (UK) Ltd*).

4 Conflicts between employees. Behaviour on the part of an employee which is causing disruption and discontent within the rest of the workforce has been held to constitute 'some other substantial reason' for dismissal.

For example, in *Treganowan* v *Robert Knee & Co Ltd*, a female employee's frequent and open boasting about her sexual exploits had created tensions within the office which were affecting business. This behaviour was held to be 'some other substantial reason' for dismissal and fair in the circumstances because she was completely insensitive to the effect she was having.

In such cases, however, dismissal must be viewed as a weapon of last resort and the employer must make sensible, practical and genuine efforts to see whether an improvement in relationships can be effected. The possibility of transferring the employee to another department should also be explored (*Turner* v *Vestric Ltd*).

Finally, it should be borne in mind that pressure for the dismissal of an employee from the rest of the workforce which takes the form of industrial action will not assist the employer in justifying the dismissal. The EPCA s63 specifically provides that, in determining the reason for the dismissal and its reasonableness, no account shall be taken of any industrial action threatened or taken against the employer.

5   Dismissal for refusal to accept changes in contractual terms resulting from a business reorganisation. One of the most controversial areas of unfair dismissal has concerned the correct approach to the situation where the employer wishes to reorganise the business in such a way that changes result in the employees' terms and condition of employment.

These changes may not fall within the legal concept of redundancy because the work that the employee does is not diminished (see *Johnson* v *Nottinghamshire Combined Police Authority* and *Lesney Products Ltd* v *Nolan*). The test of fairness is not inevitably controlled by the content of the contract of employment. As a result, the courts and tribunals have been prepared to hold as fair dismissals where the employee has refused to agree to a change in terms and conditions of employment in line with the employer's perception of business efficacy. Dismissals for refusal to agree to unilateral changes in job content, pay, location and hours of work have been held to be for 'some other substantial reason' and fair (see, for example, *Ellis* v *Brighton Co-operative Society* and *Hollister* v *NFU*).

The tribunal will expect the employer to lead evidence to show why it was felt to be necessary to impose the changes (*Banerjee* v *City and East London Area Health Authority*), and it is also material for the tribunal to know whether the company was making a profit or loss (*Ladbroke Courage Holidays Ltd* v *Asten*).

However, the courts and tribunals have not imposed particularly strict criteria when judging the 'substantiality' of the decision to reorganise. In *Ellis* (above), it was suggested that the test was whether, if the changes were not implemented, the whole business would be brought to a standstill. A much less stringent test was formulated by Lord Denning in *Hollister* (above), where he felt that the principle should extend to situations 'where there was some sound, good business reason for the reorganisation'. In subsequent cases, the EAT has been prepared to dilute the test even further – in one case requiring only that the changes were considered as 'matters of importance' or to have 'discernable advantages to the organisation' (*Banerjee* (above)), and in another demanding that the reorganisation be 'beneficial' (***Bowater Containers v McCormack***).

Surveys of the case law on reorganisation or 'business efficacy' tend to show the adoption of a strong conception of managerial prerogative by the courts and tribunals (see 'Any Other Substantial Reason: A Managerial Prerogative?' by Painter, 131 *The New Law Journal* (1981), and 'Unfair Dismissal and Managerial Prerogative: A Study of "Other Substantial Reason", by Bowers and Clark, 10 *Industrial Law Journal* 34 (1981)).

In ***Evans v Elementa Holdings***, a case involving the imposition of an obligation to work overtime, the EAT moved some way to redressing this imbalance in favour of managerial prerogative in holding that, if it was unreasonable to expect an employee to accept the changes, it was unfair for the employer to dismiss. This view, however, was not accepted by a differently constituted EAT in ***Chubb Fire Security Ltd v Harper***. In its view the correct approach, in accordance with the decision of the Court of Appeal in ***Hollister v NFU*** (above), is for the industrial tribunal to concentrate on whether it was reasonable for the employer to implement the reorganisation by terminating existing contracts and offering new ones:

'It may be perfectly reasonable for an employee to decline to work extra overtime, having regard to his family commitments. Yet from the employer's point of view, having regard to his business commitments, it may be perfectly reasonable to require an employee to work overtime.'

Some form of consultation over the reorganisation has been expected in the past in order to maintain the fairness of the dismissal. The dilution of the importance of consultation in ***Hollister*** – where the Court of Appeal held that consultation is only one of the factors to be taken into account when judging reasonableness and lack of it and would not necessarily render a dismissal unfair – should be reassessed following the decision of the House of Lords in ***Polkey*** (above).

However, having said this, there is no clear guidance on the form the consultation should take. In ***Ellis v Brighton Co-operative Society Ltd*** (above), the EAT were satisfied that the requirement of consultation had been fulfilled by union agreement to the scheme, even though Ellis, as a non-union member, had little chance of participating in the scheme. In *Martin* v *Automobile Proprietary Ltd*, however, there are suggestions that non-union members should expect to be individually consulted.

6 Dismissal on a transfer of undertaking. Regulation 8 of the Transfer of Undertakings (Protection of Employment) Regulations 1981, provides that a dismissal of an employee of the transferor or transferee which is connected with the transfer of the business is automatically unfair unless it is for an 'economic, technical or organisational reason entailing changes in the workforce' (see also chapter 4).

By virtue of reg 8(2) such dismissals are deemed to be for a substantial reason for the purpose of EPCA s57(1), and are fair provided they pass the statutory test of reasonableness. It is now clear that, if the employer does successfully establish the economic, technical or organisational (ETO) defence, an employee can claim a redundancy payment if redundancy was the reason for the transfer dismissal (*Gorictree Ltd* v *Jenkinson*).

The scope of the ETO defence was considered by the Court of Appeal in *Berriman* v *Delabole Slate Ltd*. The Court held that in order to come within reg 8(2), the employer must show that a change in the workforce is part of the economic, technical or organisational reason for dismissal. It must be an objective of the employer's plan to achieve changes in the workforce, not just a possible consequence of the plan. So where an employee resigned following a transfer because the transferee employer proposed to remove his or her guaranteed weekly wage, so as to bring pay into line with the transferee's existing workforce, the reason behind the plan was to produce uniform terms and conditions, and was not in any way to reduce the numbers in the workforce.

In *Crawford* v *Swinton Insurance Brokers Ltd*, prior to transfer of the business, Mrs Crawford was a clerk typist working mainly from home. After the transfer, she was offered other work with the changed function of selling insurance. She refused and claimed she had been constructively and unfairly dismissed. The EAT held that if, as a result of an organisational change on a relevant transfer, a workforce is engaged in a different occupation or function, there is a change of workforce for the purpose reg 8(2) and any dismissal is potentially fair.

In order to counter the effects of the decision in **Berriman**, there was a developing practice of purchasers of a business insisting that the vendor dismisses the workforce before the transfer takes place. In this way, the transferee sought to avoid any liability for unfair dismissal and/or redundancy pay in relation to the transferor's workforce. In **Anderson and another v Dalkeith Engineering Ltd**, the Scottish EAT held that a dismissal by the transferor at the behest of the transferee was an 'economic' reason and therefore fell within reg 8(2). The EAT was of the view that to get the best deal for the sale of the business, the vendor had to accede to the purchaser's demand and that was clearly an 'economic reason'.

This approach was not adopted by the English EAT in **Wheeler v Patel and J Golding Group of Companies**, where it thought that the word 'economic' should be given a more restricted meaning. It was felt that an 'economic reason' must relate to the conduct of the business. A desire to obtain an enhanced price for the business or to achieve a sale is not a reason which relates to the conduct of the business and is therefore not an economic reason. The **Wheeler** approach was subsequently supported by the EAT in **Gateway Hotels Ltd v Stewart and others**.

It is clear from the decision of the House of Lords in **Litster v Forth Dry Dock & Engineering Co Ltd** – discussed in chapter 3 – that the mere insistence of the purchaser that the vendor dismiss as a condition of sale will not be regarded as an 'economic, technical or organisational reason entailing changes in the workforce'. As a result of the **Litster** decision, where an employee has been unfairly dismissed for a reason connected with the transfer, he or she is to be deemed to have been employed in the undertaking 'immediately before the transfer' and the employment is statutorily continued with the transferee. This means that any unfair dismissal claim will be against the transferee employer.

In the light of these developments, purchasers of businesses are now well advised to deal with the question of reductions in the size of the transferor's workforce *after* the transfer is complete. At least in this way, the purchaser is in effective control of how any reduction is handled rather than seeking to defend the manner in which the vendor brought about the dismissals.

7 REMEDIES FOR UNFAIR DISMISSAL

Once the tribunal is satisfied that an employee has been unfairly dismissed, it has to consider one of three forms of remedy:

- an order for reinstatement
- an order of re-engagement
- an award of compensation (see EPCA ss67–9).

Although reinstatement and re-engagement are regarded as primary remedies by the statute, such orders are only made by tribunals in roughly 3 per cent of successful cases. In practice, compensation is the normal remedy for unfair dismissal. As a result, the re-employment of dismissed employees has been described as 'the lost remedy'. A major weakness, from the employee's point of view, is the fact that the industrial tribunal cannot force an employer to take back a dismissed employee. Where an order for reinstatement/re-engagement is made but the employer does not comply, the applicant can only seek compensation which will be enhanced to reflect, albeit in some limited sense, the employer's failure to comply.

This point is graphically illustrated in ***O'Laoire v Jackel International Ltd***. An industrial tribunal, as part of an order for reinstatement, specified that the applicant should receive a sum totalling £27,833 gross, representing back pay between the date of the dismissal and the date of reinstatement. The employers refused to comply with the order and he was awarded compensation of £12,185 (including an additional award) which was maximum which at that time could be awarded at that time, given the statutory limit on unfair dismissal compensation awards. His actual losses, as found by the industrial tribunal, exceeded £100,000.

The applicant then sought to enforce in the county court the provisions relating to back pay set out in the re-instatement order. The Court of Appeal held that such an action was not available to the applicant. A reinstatement order is wholly unenforceable. If such an order is not complied with, whether wholly or in part, the applicant's only remedy is to apply to the industrial tribunal for compensation. The monetary provisions of a reinstatement order do not create a cause of action enforceable through the county courts.

Noting the injustice of the position in the case of higher paid employees, the Master of the Rolls expressed the view that the present maximum level of compensation for unfair dismissal can positively discourage employers from complying with an order for reinstatement. He felt the time had arrived for a fundamental review of the compensation limits.

The principles governing the normal remedies are set out below together with the special rules and procedures concerning trade union related dismissals.

Reinstatement or re-engagement

On finding a complaint well-founded, the industrial tribunal must explain to the applicant the availability of the orders of reinstatement or re-engagement and ask whether he or she wishes the tribunal to make such an order. Assuming that the applicant wishes to be reinstated or re-engaged, the industrial tribunal must then take the following additional factors into account in exercising its discretion:

- whether it is practicable for an employer to comply with such an order *and*
- whether the employee caused or contributed to his or her dismissal and, if so, whether it would be just and equitable to make the order.

An order for reinstatement is an order that the employer shall treat the applicant in all respects as if he or she had not been dismissed, and on making such an order the tribunal shall specify:

1　Any amounts payable to the employee in respect of any benefit which the employee might have received but for the dismissal, including arrears of pay, for the period from the date of termination to the date of reinstatement, including any benefits which the employee might have enjoyed by way of improvements in terms and conditions but for the dismissal.

2　Any rights and privileges, including seniority and pension rights, which must be restored to the employee.

3 The date by which the order must be complied with.

Only if the industrial tribunal decides not to make an order to reinstate the employee in his or her old job should it then go on to consider the question of re-engagement.

An order for re-engagement is defined as an order that the applicant be engaged by the employer, or by a successor of the employer or by an associated employer, in employment comparable to that from which he or she was dismissed, or other suitable employment. It will be appreciated that this is a much more flexible remedy.

An order must specify:

- the employer's identity
- the nature of the employer
- the remuneration for the employment
- any amount payable by the employer to the employee in respect of any benefit which the applicant might reasonably be expected to have received but for the dismissal, including arrears of pay, for the period between the date of termination of employment and the date of re-engagement
- any rights and privileges, including seniority and pension rights, which must be restored to the employee
- the date by which the order must be complied with (EPCA s69).

In *City & Hackney Health Authority* v *Crisp*, the question arose as to whether the industrial tribunal has power to reduce the amount payable by an employer in respect of arrears of pay between the date of termination and the date of reinstatement/re-engagement, on the grounds that the employee has not effectively mitigated his or her loss. It was alleged by the employers in this case that Mrs Crisp had not mitigated her loss because she had waited over two months after her dismissal before taking steps to claim unfair dismissal. If she had acted earlier, it was argued, she would have been re-engaged at an earlier date and the back pay would have been correspondingly smaller.

The EAT rejected this argument. An order for reinstatement under s69(2) must require the employer to 'treat the complainant in all respects as if he had not been dismissed' and an order for re-engagement must be on terms which, in accordance with s69(6), 'are as favourable as an order for reinstatement'. As a result, there were no grounds for implying a duty to mitigate loss into re-engagement provisions. Moreover, the EAT expressed the opinion that it doubted whether an employee's dilatoriness in pursuing an unfair dismissal claim could amount to a failure to mitigate where, as in the present case, notwithstanding that dilatoriness the complaint was presented within the three month statutory time limit.

Is it practicable to reinstate or re-engage?

An employer will not be able to argue that it is not practicable to reinstate/re-engage the employee because a replacement employee has been engaged unless he or she can show either:

- that it was not practicable to arrange for the dismissed employee's work to be done without employing a permanent replacement *or*
- that the replacement was engaged after the lapse of a reasonable period of time, without having heard from the dismissed employee that he or she wished to be reinstated or re-engaged; it no longer being reasonable for the employer to have the dismissed employee's work carried out by anyone except a permanent replacement (EPCA s70(1)).

Failure to comply with an order for reinstatement or re-engagement

Where an order is made and the employee is taken back but the employer does not comply fully with its terms, the tribunal will make such an award of compensation as it thinks fit having regard to the loss sustained by the applicant in consequence of the partial failure to comply with the order (EPCA s71(1)).

In the more frequent situation of a total failure to comply with the order, the tribunal will award compensation using the normal rules of computation plus an 'additional award' (see below). It is a defence to the granting of the additional award if the employer can show that it was not practicable to comply with the order.

Impracticability is therefore a possible defence at two stages in the process of industrial tribunal decision-making. The following circumstances have been held to render a reinstatement/re-engagement impracticable:

- Where it would inevitably lead to industrial strife (*Coleman* v *Magnet Joinery Ltd*).
- Where there is no suitable vacancy. A re-engagement order does not place a duty on the employer to search for and find work for the dismissed employee irrespective of existing vacancies (*Freemans plc* v *Flynn*).
- Where the employee believes him or herself to be a victim of conspiracy by the employers, he or she is not likely to be a satisfactory employee in any circumstances if reinstated or re-engaged (*Nothman* v *London Borough of Barnet (No 2)*).
- Where there must exist a close personal relationship, reinstatement can only be appropriate in exceptional circumstances and to enforce it upon a reluctant employer is not a course which an industrial tribunal should pursue unless persuaded by powerful evidence that it would succeed (*Enessy Co SA (trading as The Tulchan Estate)* v *Minoprio and Minoprio*).

Compensation

The rules relating to the calculation of unfair dismissal compensation can be summarised as follows:

The basic award

The basic award (EPCA s73) is an award of half, one, or one and a half weeks' pay for each year of continuous service (depending on age), subject to a maximum of 20 years. A week's pay is calculated in accordance with EPCA sch 14 and is based on gross pay. The maximum allowable for a week's pay is currently £198 (1991–2) – this figure is reviewed each year and any changes made operate from April.

If aged	But less than	No of weeks' pay for each year
–	22	½
22	41	1
41	65	1½

Therefore, in general, the maximum payment under this head of calculation in the year 1991–2 will be:

£198 × 20 × 1½ = £5,940

Retention of minimum award

The basic award used to be subject to a minimum award of two weeks' pay but this was abolished by the Employment Act 1980. Therefore, given the operation of the deduction provisions set out below, it is possible for a tribunal to reduce the basic award to nil. However, there are two situations where a minimum award is still maintained:

1 Where the industrial tribunal finds that the reason or principal reason for the dismissal was redundancy, but

 • the employee refused or left suitable alternative employment
 or
 • the employee's contract was renewed or he or she was re-engaged within four weeks,

 the employee will be entitled to a basic award of two weeks' pay (EPCA s73(2)). This is despite the fact that he or she would not be considered to be dismissed for the purposes of claiming statutory redundancy payments.

2 Where the dismissal is regarded as 'automatically unfair' because it is related to membership/non-membership of a trade union or union activity under EPCA s58 or s59(a), the basic award (before any reduction for reasons set out below) will be a minimum of £2,650 in 1991–2, and is subject to annual review.

Deductions from the basic award

Deductions can be made from the basic award in certain circumstances and are calculated as follows:

- If the applicant is aged 64, entitlement goes down one-twelfth for each month after his or her 64th birthday. For example, an employee aged 64 years and 6 months would have his or her basic award reduced by six-twelfths or halved (EPCA s73(5)(6)).
- Where the applicant has received a redundancy payment, whether under the statutory or a private scheme, the basic award will be reduced by the amount of that payment (EPCA s73(9)).
- Where the employee has unreasonably refused an offer of re-instatement by the employer, the basic award will be reduced by an amount which the tribunal considers just and equitable (EPCA s73(7)(A).
- Where the employer makes an ex gratia payment which is specifi-cally intended to cover any liability to compensation which, if large enough, may also be set off against any entitlement to a compen-satory award (see *Chelsea Football Club and Athletic Co Ltd* v *Heath*).
- Where the tribunal considers that any conduct of the applicant before the dismissal (or, where the dismissal was with notice, before the notice was given), was such that it would be just and equitable to reduce the basic award (EPCA s73(7)(B)), it may do so.

The compensatory award

The tribunal may also make a compensatory award (EPCA s74). This is an 'amount which the tribunal considers just and equitable in all the circumstances having regard to the loss sustained by the complainant in consequence of the dismissal in so far as that loss is attributable to action taken by the employer' (EPCA s74(1)). The maximum award under this head is currently £10,000.

The aim of the award is to reimburse the employee for any financial loss experienced; it is not to punish the employer for poor personnel practices (see *Clarkson International Tools Ltd* v *Short*). It follows, therefore, that if the employee has in fact suffered no loss then he or she should receive a nil compensatory award. The decision of the

House of Lords in **Polkey v AE Dayton Services Ltd** has already been discussed, where it was held that a dismissal could not be held to be substantively fair merely because with hindsight a procedural lapse would not have made any difference to the outcome. However, the reasoning of their Lordships in **Polkey** fully accepts the position that if failures in procedure would not have prevented the dismissal taking place then this should be reflected in the level of the compensatory award.

Norton Tool Co v Tewson, one of the earliest unfair dismissal cases, still provides valuable guidance to industrial tribunals in considering a compensatory award. In this case it was said that the general principles for calculating unfair dismissal are twofold:

1   to compensate fully but not to award a bonus

2   the amount to be awarded is what is just and equitable having regard to the loss sustained by the applicant.

Loss in this context does not include injury to feelings. The burden of proving loss lies with the applicant. The industrial tribunal has a duty to set out its reasoning in sufficient detail in order to show the principles on which it proceeded.

The court in **Norton Tool** stated that an award of unfair dismissal compensation should include the following heads of damage:

- immediate loss of wages
- future loss of wages
- loss arising from the manner of dismissal
- loss of protection in respect of unfair dismissal.

Immediate loss of wages

This represents loss of net earnings from the date of dismissal until the date of the hearing. For the purpose of this calculation there is no limit on the amount of the weekly wage as there is when the basic award is calculated.

The tribunal will take account of wages paid in lieu of notice and earnings in other employments, and set these payments off against the compensation otherwise payable under this head. The one exception to this principle of deduction is where the employee receives earnings from a new employment during what should have been his or her notice period with the former employer – in this case the amount earned will not normally be deducted from compensation (see **Babcock FATA Ltd v Addison**).

Where a new job has been obtained, the normal rule is that the tribunal should assess what the applicant would have earned from the respondent employer *up to the date of the hearing on compensation*, giving credit for any earnings from new employment (**Ging v Ellward (Lancs) Ltd**). However, the operation of the normal rule has the potential for injustice if the employee obtains a higher paid job and there is a lengthy period between the dismissal and the date of the hearing on compensation. In such circumstances, the size of the award will decrease daily and the set-off from the higher paid job could ultimately swallow the compensatory award completely. This problem was recognised by the EAT in **Fentiman v Fluid Engineering Products**.

In this case, Mr Fentiman was dismissed by the respondent company on 12 April 1989. On 5 November 1989 he obtained new employment at a significantly higher rate of pay than he had received from his former employers.

An industrial tribunal upheld Mr Fentiman's claim for unfair dismissal. They assessed his compensatory award on the basis of the loss of his earnings from the date his employment terminated, to the date that the industrial tribunal's decision on compensation was promulgated, 6 August 1990, less the earnings from his new employment during that period. That produced a net loss of £2,373. On appeal, it was successfully argued on Mr Fentiman's behalf that the compensatory award should have been assessed on his loss of earnings from the date his employment with the respondents terminated until the date he took up his new employment, that being the date on which the loss attributable to his dismissal ceased. On that basis, the EAT held that his actual loss was £9,744.

The EAT expressed the view that the normal rule laid down in **Ging** was satisfactory when the differences in the wages between the old and new jobs are minimal. But where, as in **Fentiman**, there is a combination of factors such as a greatly increased wage in the second employment and a lengthy period of time between dismissal and hearing, the normal rule does not produce a 'just and equitable' result. In such circumstances, the industrial tribunal should decide whether the employment is permanent and, if so, calculate the loss as between the date of dismissal and the obtaining of the new employment. Any other approach would result in the employer who unfairly dismissed paying compensation in respect of only a fraction of the loss sustained by the employee during a period of unemployment.

Loss of fringe benefits such as company car, private health care, low interest loan, subsidised accommodation will also be taken into account in assessing compensation for both past and future loss. The EPCA s74(2) makes specific reference to the inclusion of 'any expenses reasonably incurred by the complainant in consequence of the dismissal'. This might include the expenses incurred in looking for alternative employment, but does not include the legal costs involved in bringing the unfair dismissal action.

Future loss of wages

Where the applicant is still without a job at the date of the hearing or has taken a job which is at a lower wage, the industrial tribunal will have to embark on a highly speculative exercise of forecasting the future losses which the applicant is likely to sustain, including wages, pensions and other fringe benefits. Given that assessment of future loss can only be an approximation, and the fact that the statute gives a wide discretion to the industrial tribunal, an award will not be overturned on appeal unless clearly misguided.

The loss of non-transferable pension rights on dismissal can be substantial. In *Copson v Eversure Accessories Ltd*, two types of loss were identified:

1   loss of the pension earned up to the date of dismissal, eg 15 years' service towards a pension of £X in 20 years' time at the age of 65 *and*

2   the individual's loss of future opportunity to improve on his or her pension position, ie the opportunity of improving his or her position until the time at which the pension becomes payable.

The loss of present pension position can also be substantial. One approach to the assessment of loss under this head is to assess it in terms of loss of contributions. In *Copson*, it was said:

'Properly funded pensions are built up by the payment of periodical contributions by employers and usually also by employees. These contributions are invested under favourable taxation provisions and built up to a capital sum which at retirement age will buy an annuity equal to the amount of the pension. Thus, a rough assessment of the accrued value of a worker's pension position at any point in time can be achieved by taking the sum of the pension already paid increased by compound interest from the date of payment. The calculation of compound interest is not easy without tables, but an increase in the rate of simple interest applied to the capital sum will achieve a rough and ready justice . . . If the claimant is dismissed shortly before he reaches pensionable age, an alternative approach is to take the capital value of the pension to which he would have become entitled and to discount it for accelerated payment.'

Certain discounts should then be made from the total value of the employee's pension based on contributions. Where the employer or pension fund has repaid the employee's contributions with or without interest, credit must be given for this repayment. In addition, certain employees will lose the benefit of pensionable service without any fault on the part of the employer. For example, if the employee would have later resigned or been fairly dismissed had he or she not already been unfairly dismissed, he or she has lost nothing. Finally, where the employee on dismissal becomes entitled to a paid up pension payable on retirement or has the right to transfer his or her pension, the loss under this head may be nil.

The loss of future pension opportunities also has to be considered. If the unfairly dismissed employee can continue to improve his or her pension position in any new employment at the same rate of benefit and at no greater personal cost, there is no loss under this head. But this will rarely be the case. Even where the employee finds new pensionable employment, the industrial tribunal may well need to assess the loss of the former employer's contributions during any period of unemployment betweeen the old and new job. Where the pension scheme in the new employment has a lower rate of benefit than that operating in the former employment, this too must also be taken into account. Where the new job has no pension entitlement, this can be assessed by taking the former employer's contributions that would have been made to the fund in respect of the period for which the anticipated loss is expected to persist.

Having assessed prima facie loss, however, it is not appropriate for the industrial tribunal merely to multiply that figure by the number of years left to retirement age; to do so would take no account of the various contingencies such as death, resignation or dismissal which might occur before that time. These contingencies should be discounted against prima facie loss by the employment of a multiplier to take these and other factors into account.

Given the complexities and uncertainties surrounding loss of pension rights, a document was drawn up in 1980 by the Government Actuary's Department for the guidance of industrial tribunals. In 1990, this document was replaced by a new set of guidelines prepared by a committee of Industrial Tribunal Chairs in consultation with the Actuary's Department, entitled *Industrial Tribunals: Compensation for loss of pension rights* (HMSO). The booklet gives general guidance on several aspects of pension loss with specific advice on the three main heads of loss:

- loss of pension rights from the date of the dismissal to the date of hearing
- loss of future rights
- loss of enhancement of accrued rights.

The authors of the booklet emphasise that they are only offering guidelines and that it is always open to the parties to present their own actuarial assessments. Nevertheless, in this area of uncertainty the booklet will undoubtedly be very influential.

Loss arising from the manner of dismissal

As is the case with the common law action for wrongful dismissal, no account will be taken of injury to feelings in assessing the compensatory award. However, there may be the exceptional case where the manner of the dismissal has had a tangible effect on the applicant's future employment prospects (eg by damaging his or her reputation in the trade or industry) and in such a case compensation may be claimed under this head (see *Vaughan* v *Weighpack Ltd*).

Loss of protection in respect of unfair dismissal

Where the employee is dismissed he or she will have to 'start from scratch' in terms of building the necessary periods of continuous employment required to claim unfair dismissal and redundancy payment rights in the future. As a result, the tribunal will normally award a nominal sum to compensate for the loss of this protection. In *S H Muffett Ltd* v *Head*, the appropriate figure was assessed to be normally £100.

Deductions from the compensatory award

Contributory fault

Where the tribunal finds that the dismissal was to any extent caused or contributed to by any action of the applicant, it shall reduce the compensatory award by such proportion as it considers just and equitable having regard to that finding (EPCA s74(6)). Normally, the same percentage deduction will apply to both basic and compensatory awards (*RSPCA* v *Cruden*).

If the employee is found to have contributed to the dismissal, the award of compensation may be reduced by as much as 100 per cent (*W Devis & Sons Ltd* v *Atkins*).

In *Nelson* v *BBC (No 2)*, the Court of Appeal suggested that the industrial tribunal adopt a three stage approach in considering the question of contributory fault:

1   There must be a finding that there was conduct on the part of the employee in connection with the dismissal which was culpable or blameworthy. It 'does not necessarily have to involve conduct amounting to a breach of contract or a tort. It ... also includes conduct which while not amounting to a breach of contract or a tort is nevertheless perverse or foolish or bloody minded. It may also include conduct which though not meriting any of those more pejorative epithets, is nevertheless unacceptable in the circumstances.'

2   There must be a finding that this conduct actually caused or contributed to the unfair dismissal.

3   There must be a finding that it is just and equitable to reduce the
    assessment of the applicant's loss to a specified extent.

It is easy to envisage the rules on contributory fault operating in
cases of misconduct but can they also apply in cases of dismissal by
reasons of capability? Conflicting answers have been given to this
question. In *Kraft Foods Ltd v Fox*, it was held that where employees
are doing their best and their best is not good enough, it would be
wrong to reduce compensation on the basis of contributory fault.

However, in *Moncur v International Paint Co Ltd*, it was doubted
whether an act or failing which is attributable to a defect of character
or personality of the claimant, and which is not within his or her
control to alter, can never be material when deciding the contributory
fault. This approach has now received the approval of the EAT in
Finnie v Top Hat Frozen Foods Ltd.

While there is some doubt, therefore, about whether contributory
fault is applicable in every type of dismissal based on lack of capability, it
is clear that the principle of contribution *will* apply where the employee
was incapable of doing the job because of laziness, negligence or
idleness (see *Sutton & Gates (Luton) Ltd v Boxall*).

Mitigation

Under EPCA s74(4), applicants are under the same duty to take
reasonable steps to mitigate their loss as would apply at common law.
So, they must make reasonable attempts to obtain alternative employment. Unreasonable refusal of an offer of reinstatement by the same
employer may amount to a failure to mitigate (*Sweetlove v Redbridge
and Waltham Forest Area Health Authority*).

As stated in chapter 4, there is an unresolved conflict as to whether
a failure to invoke a right of appeal amounts to a failure to take
reasonable steps to mitigate loss, allowing the industrial tribunal to
reduce compensation accordingly (see *Hoover Ltd v Forde*, which
favours this approach and the decision of the Scottish EAT in
William Muir (Bond 9) Ltd v Lamb, which comes out strongly
against it).

Where the employer is able to establish that the applicant has failed
to mitigate loss, this can result in reduction of the compensatory
award.

Payments made by the employer

Any ex gratia payment made by the employer will be deducted from the compensatory award. EPCA s75(3) makes it clear that the amount of the ex gratia payment must be taken into account *before* the statutory maximum (currently £10,000) is applied (see ***McCarthy* v *British Insulated Callenders Cables***).

Similarly, the statutory maximum will only be imposed after the deduction of the percentage determined for contributory fault. On this basis, it is still possible for applicants to receive a maximum compensatory award despite being held to have contributed to their own dismissal. There is a conflict of authority as to whether payments made by the employer to the applicant should be deducted before or after deductions for contributory fault (***Clement-Clarke International Ltd* v *Manley*** compared with ***UBAF Bank Ltd* v *Davis***).

Recoupment of unemployment benefit and income support

In calculating compensation for unfair dismissal, industrial tribunals no longer deduct sums – as they did prior to 1977 – in respect of unemployment benefit or income support which the applicant may have received from the Department of Employment or the DSS. Under the Employment Protection (Recoupment of Unemployment Benefit and Supplementary Benefit) Regulations 1977 (SI 1977 No 674), the tribunal, when making an award of compensation, must identify the 'prescribed element' of the award. This element represents the amount of the compensatory award which is attributable to the loss of earnings between date of termination and the end of the tribunal proceedings.

This part of the award must then be withheld from the applicant by the former employer. The Department of Employment will then serve on the employer a recoupment notice which requires the employer to pay back to them from the 'prescribed element' an amount representing any social security benefits which have been paid to the employee. Once this has been done, the balance of the 'prescribed element' must be paid by the employer to the successful applicant. The Recoupment Regulations only apply where unemployment benefit or income support was actually claimed during the period.

In assessing future loss, the tribunal does not have to take into account the possibility of the receipt of future benefits by the applicant.

Where compensation is based on unemployment for X weeks, for example, then the applicant is disqualified from receipt of benefit during this period (see the Social Security (Unemployment, Sickness and Invalidity Benefit) Regulations 1983 (SI 1983 No 1598) reg 7(1)(K) and the Income Support (General) Regulations 1987 (SI 1987 No 1967) reg 35 (1)(b)).

The additional award

This award is made where an order for reinstatement or re-engagement is not complied with. If the original dismissal was for a reason other than sex or race discrimination, the award may be between 13 and 26 weeks' pay (maximum 26 × 198 = £5,148). If the reason was for discrimination, then there is a discretion to award between 26 and 52 weeks' pay (maximum 52 × 198 = £10,296).

The special award in union related dismissals

By virtue of amendments introduced by the Employment Act 1982, the amount of compensation to be awarded to employees who are unfairly dismissed (or selected for redundancy) on grounds of trade union membership and activities or non-membership, is much higher than for other types of dismissal because a 'special award' is made in addition to the basic and compensatory awards (see EPCA s75A).

The special award can be made *only* where the applicant requests the industrial tribunal to make an order for reinstatement or re-engagement (EPCA s72(c)). Where reinstatement/re-engagement is sought by the dismissed employee, there are two different levels of compensation laid down depending on the following two circumstances:

1 Where reinstatement/re-engagement is requested but no such order is made by the industrial tribunal under the discretionary powers vested in it by EPCA s69. If this is the case, then the *special award* will comprise:

   104 weeks' pay subject to a minimum of £13,180 and a maximum of £26,290.

2   Where reinstatement/re-engagement is ordered by the industrial tribunal but the order is not complied with. In this instance, unless the employer can satisfy the tribunal that it was not practicable to comply with the order, the *special award* will be:

156 weeks' pay subject to a minimum of £19,735 and *no maximum figure.*

Where the tribunal is satisfied that it was not practicable for the employer to comply with the original order, the compensation will be as under 1 above.

In common with the other compensation limits, the levels of the special award are reviewed annually by the Secretary of State. Unlike the basic and compensatory awards, a week's pay for the purposes of the special award is not subject to any statutory limit.

The special award may be reduced by a tribunal where it feels that it is just and equitable to do so because of the employee's conduct before the dismissal, or that the employee had in some way obstructed the employer's attempt to comply with the reinstatement/re-engagement order. However, EPCA s72A makes it clear that the tribunals should disregard certain types of conduct by the employee when considering the level of the award. These are:

- any breach by the employee of an undertaking to become a member of a trade union or of a particular trade union, to cease to be a member of a trade union or of a particular trade union or not to take part in the activities of any trade union or of a particular trade union
- any breach of an undertaking to make a payment in lieu of union membership, or any objection to the employer making a deduction from his or her wages to cover payments in lieu.

Union liability for compensation

The EPCA s76A allows for either the employer or the applicant to request that a trade union or other party be joined in the proceedings where they have exerted or threatened to exert industrial pressure on the employer to dismiss. Such a request must be granted if it is made before the hearing begins, but may be refused if it is made after that time. No request for joinder will be entertained after the tribunal has made an award of compensation or an order for reinstatement/re-engagement.

If the tribunal finds the complaint of third party pressure well-founded, the industrial tribunal has the power to order that the trade union or other party pay any or all of the compensation awarded.

Interim relief in respect of trade union related dismissals

An employee who alleges that he or she has been dismissed for union/non-union membership or trade union activities can apply to the tribunal for an order for *interim relief* (EPCA s77(1)).

The order for interim relief is intended to preserve the status quo until the full hearing of these cases, which by their very nature can be extremely damaging to the industrial relations climate of any organisation. Where relief is granted it will result in either the reinstatement/re-engagement of the employee pending full hearing or, in some cases, a suspension of the employee on continued terms and conditions.

Three conditions must be satisfied before an order for interim relief will be made:

1   The application must be presented to the tribunal before the end of the period of seven days immediately following the 'effective date of termination'.

2   Where the allegation relates to dismissal for trade union membership or taking part in union activities, there must also be presented to the tribunal within the same seven day period a certificate signed by an authorised official of the union concerned. This certificate should state that in the official's opinion there appear to be reasonable grounds for the allegation. Having received the application, supported by the certificate, the tribunal must hear the application 'as soon as practicable', though giving at least seven days' notice of hearing to the employer.

3   It must appear to the tribunal 'likely' that the complaint will succeed at full hearing.

If these conditions are satisfied, the tribunal must ask the employer whether he or she is willing to reinstate or re-engage the employee. If the employer is not willing, then the tribunal must make an order for the continuation of the employee's contract of employment. This means that the contract of employment will continue in force until the full hearing as if it had not been terminated. During that period the pay or any other benefits derived from the employment, seniority, pension rights, etc and continuity of employment will be preserved.

Non-compliance with an order for interim relief

Where the employer fails to comply with an interim relief order for reinstatement or re-engagement, the tribunal must:

- make an order for the continuation of the contract *and*
- order the employer to pay the employee such compensation as the tribunal considers just and equitable having regard to the failure to comply and the loss suffered by the employee as a result.

If the employer fails to observe the terms of a continuation order then:

- if non-compliance consists of a failure to pay an amount specified in the order, the tribunal shall determine the amount owed
- in any other case of non-compliance, the tribunal shall order the employer to pay the employee such compensation as the tribunal considers just and equitable in all the circumstances.

INDEX